Language and Security

STUDIES IN LINGUISTICS, ANGLOPHONE LITERATURES AND CULTURES

Edited by Robert Kiełtyka and Agnieszka Uberman

VOLUME 41

Irina Dulebová / Radoslav Štefančík / Nina Cingerová

Language and Security
The Language of Securitization in Contemporary Slovak Public Discourse

Translated by Mgr. Beáta Biliková, PhD.
Proofread by Paul McCullough

PETER LANG

Berlin - Lausanne - Bruxelles - Chennai - New York - Oxford

Bibliographic Information published by the Deutsche Nationalbibliothek
The Deutsche Nationalbibliothek lists this publication in the Deutsche Nationalbibliografie; detailed bibliographic data is available online at http://dnb.d-nb.de.

Library of Congress Cataloging-in-Publication Data
A CIP catalog record for this book has been applied for at the Library of Congress.

Cover illustration: Courtesy of Benjamin Ben Chaim

The monograph is a result of the research project VEGA 1/0452/21
Jazyk sekuritizácie v súčasnom slovenskom verejnom diskurze -
The Language of Securitization in Contemporary Slovak Public Discourse.

ISSN 2364-7558
ISBN 978-3-631-91368-0 (Print)
E-ISBN 978-3-631-91847-0 (E-PDF)
E-ISBN 978-3-631-91848-7 (EPUB)
DOI 10.3726/b21851

© 2024 Peter Lang Group AG, Lausanne

Published by Peter Lang GmbH, Berlin, Germany

info@peterlang.com - www.peterlang.com

Contents

Introduction

In the information war of the 21st century, which is gaining momentum, not only real but imaginary fabricated threats often act as arguments in the process of persuasion, and are articulated with the primary aim of creating in the recipients a sense of acute danger to various areas of their existence (their personality, their family, their social group, their nation and various other entities with which they identify and whose status determines the standards of their life). The continuous inducing of a sense of threat is the easiest and most effective method of manipulation because it encourages the listener to "switch off" reason and "switch on" emotions. The sense of threat evoked by an experienced political or media actor leads the recipients of the message (potential voters) to make hasty judgements and decisions based on feelings and emotions, as emotional reactions to the stimulus of the presented threat are often the first responses that accompany the processing and assessment of information and the subsequent action. "If we stop to consider just how much variance in the course of our lives is controlled by cognitive processes and how much by affect, and how much the one and the other influence the important outcomes in our lives, we cannot but agree that affective phenomena deserve far more attention."[1] Instilling a sense of threat and arousing negative emotions is accomplished through language, and therefore the main goal of our research is to analyse the speech acts in Slovak public discourse by prominent actors who present fabricated social threats to a wide audience in order to achieve their political goals.

The interdisciplinary research presented in this monograph is situated at the interface of political science and linguistics and thematically builds on previous correlated research by the authors' team published in the form of scientific articles and monographs (*Language and Politics*[2]; *Language and Conflict*[3]), as well as the university textbook *Political Linguistics*[4]. The books were published by the university publishing houses in Slovak language.

1   Zajonc, R. B. (1980). Feeling and thinking: Preferences need no inferences. *American Psychologist, 35*, 151–175.
2   Štefančík, R., & Dulebová, I. (2017). *Jazyk a politika. Jazyk politiky v konfliktnej štruktúre spoločnosti.* Bratislava: Ekonóm
3   Cingerová, N., & Dulebová, I. (2019). *Jazyk a konflikt. My a tí druhí v ruskom verejnom diskurze.* Bratislava: Univerzita Komenského v Bratislave.
4   Cingerová, N., Dulebová, I., & Štefančík, R. (2021). *Politická lingvistika.* Bratislava: Ekonóm.

The research draws heavily on the concept of Critical Security Studies – or securitization theory, which is based on speech act theory and focuses on the perception and conceptualization of security. In addition to the foundations of the Copenhagen School of Security Studies, we draw on approaches developed in political linguistics and discourse-oriented research.

Our attention is focussed on Slovak public discourse concerning security, manifested predominantly in the media and on social networks during the turbulent period since 2014, which has been marked by significant discursive events presented as threats (the refugee crisis in the EU, the Ukrainian crisis after the annexation of Crimea, Brexit, the COVID-19 pandemic and the associated vaccination, the war in Ukraine and its "consequences" for Slovakia, the economic crisis, Slovakia's energy dependence). We believe that the continuous articulation of these events as hypertrophied threats has become one of the key causes of the rise of Euroscepticism, isolationist tendencies and extremist sentiments in Slovak society.

In our research, we logically examined the question of what is construed as an entity in danger in Slovak public discourse, but the main goal of our research was to understand and identify the linguistic mechanism of the process. The research is innovative both in its theoretical aspect (presenting perspectives of the application of the foundations and concepts of securitization theory in the process of the lexical analysis of hate speech) and in its applied aspect. The theoretical chapter is followed by case studies analysing the discourse of prominent Slovak political actors of securitization, mainly anti-European and pro-Russian, Slovak left-wing and right-wing extremists, as well as by conspiratorial and disinformation media.

The case studies feature an analytical treatment of representative fragments of public discourse thematizing numerous "threats" to Slovak society, including the aforementioned socio-political events, a politolinguistic interpretation of the employed linguistic devices and an analysis of securitizing speech acts.

The politolinguistic and discursive vector of our research does not allow us to delve into the complex area of the psychological aspects of the security phenomenon (related to cognitive linguistics), but the opinion of an expert in the field is consonant with the premises of our research: "When I started reading about the psychology of security, I quickly realized that this research can be used both for good and for evil. The good way to use this research is to figure out how humans' feelings of security can better match the reality of security. In other words, how do we get people to recognize that they need to question their default behaviour? Giving them more information seems not to be the answer; we're already drowning in information, and these heuristics are not based on a lack of information. Perhaps by understanding how our brains process risk, and the heuristics and biases we use to think about security, we can learn how to override our natural tendencies and make better security trade-offs. Perhaps we can learn how not to be taken in by security theater, and how to convince others not to be taken in by the same".[5]

In terms of this idea, it is important to point out that the research objective of the publication is not to determine whether something is justifiably or unjustifiably articulated as a security threat. The aim is to investigate what is being modelled as a security threat in the spirit of social constructivism, how alleged threats are verbalized, which linguistic devices the disseminators of threat articulations most frequently use in presenting them, and the anticipated pragmatic effects of their use.

We have addressed this topic with the conviction of its exceptional topicality and because the growing level of available Internet technology in Slovakia is actively exploited by the promoters of various creatively-fabricated threats, which serve their political purposes and are an extremely productive means of waging information wars and disinformation campaigns. Social and political tensions in Slovak society are growing, and in this context the idea that "presenting dangers to a particular community becomes the most convenient and appropriate form of the ideology of consolidation, that is, of creating equivalence between different universal meanings and of creating a unified, internally non-contradictory identity" is relevant.[6]

We would like to thank Ing. Vladimír Benko, PhD, from the Ľ. Štúr Institute of Linguistics, who provided us with consultations in the field of corpus linguistics and created corpora for our research.

---

5   Schneier, B. (2008). The psychology of security. In S. Vaudenay (Ed.), *AFRICACRYPT 2008. AFRICACRYPT 2008. Lecture Notes in Computer Science* (pp. 50–79). Berlin, Heidelberg: Springer-Verlag.

6   Morozov, V. (2009). *Rossia i drugie: identichnost i granicy politicheskogo soobshchestva.* Moskva: NLO.

I. Securitization theory of the Copenhagen school from the perspective of discourse analysis and political linguistics

The use of discourse theory to reconceptualize the notion of security has become a current trend of scientific research at the interface of linguistics and political science at the beginning of the 21st century. In addition to a number of objective factors that have influenced the establishment of a given vector in scientific research, a significant role has also been played by the growing dissatisfaction of social science and humanities scholars with the epistemological and metatheoretical consequences of the hegemony of the military and (more broadly) state-centric paradigms in the treatment of the phenomenon of security. Linguistic discourse theories which permit the analysis of a given issue in a broader social context, in terms of the interaction between the domain of language and the domain of society, between word and action, have become more desirable. From a linguistic perspective, every social act is also seen as a linguistic act, since both individual and collective subjects must be voiced, and objective reality must be retold in order to be reproduced or transformed. Thus, language becomes important in terms of ontology[7], and from the viewpoint of a way of describing reality, language comes to be rightly seen as a way of creating, constructing and objectifying reality, i.e., as discourse.

The turn towards discourse in security research also stemmed from one of the fundamental premises of poststructuralism, according to which material objects and structures acquire their materiality and objective ontological status through discourse representation.[8] Another point of importance was the linguistic turn in social theory from reality to textuality, since the textualization of analysis implies the recognition that any reality is mediated and determined by a mode of representation, and that representations are not merely descriptions of a world of facts, but a way of producing those facts.[9] The notion of safety has thus been

---

7   Hansen, L. (2006). *Security as Practice. Discourse Analysis and the Bosnian War.* London, New York: Routledge.

8   Laclau, E., & Mouffe, C. (1985). *Hegemony and Socialist Strategy.* London: Verso, p. 108.

9   Shapiro, M. J. (1989). Textualizing global politics. In J. Der Derian, & J. M. Shapiro (Eds.), *International/Intertextual Relations: Postmodern Readings of World Politics* (pp. 11–23). New York: Lexington Books.

transposed into the field of linguistics as the linguistic choice of the producer of a speech act. As a result of the aforementioned shift in the research paradigm, security has come to be conceptualized as a speech act through which certain actors, processes, and events are presented as potential dangers to a particular entity, most often a state or a social group.[10]

In this chapter, we analyse the innovative premises of Copenhagen School theory as an impetus and opportunity to reinterpret the concept of security from the position of political linguistics and discourse analysis, allowing us to conceptualize security as a discursive practice constituting a political community. Our theoretical reflections are supplemented with significant examples from contemporary Slovak public discourse. We draw on the view of the Copenhagen School according to which the act of securitization as a speech act creates new meanings and is capable of setting in motion certain social dynamics. The primary aim of the research is to analyse how a sense of threat is created and disseminated through a speech act.

1.1 Securitization theory of the Copenhagen school

Nowadays, security is a frequent research topic in political science and other social sciences. Examples of conceptual analyses of security in political science include David Baldwin's *The Concept of Security*, which views security as a low probability of harm to existing.[11] Political scientist Richard Ullman, in *Redefining Security*, considers security to be a reduction in human vulnerability and emphasizes that non-military threats, including environmental threats, have the same or even greater potential to harm national security than conventional military threats. He proposes that the security policy agenda be re-evaluated, since non-military aspects are likely to become less manageable and the danger of neglecting them is increasing.[12] However, despite the multitude of diverse definitions, it is still a relatively poorly conceptualized framework that raises fundamental questions: who is the object of security (individuals, groups, nations, states, regions, humanity)? What are the instruments for maintaining security (military, political, economic, diplomatic, cultural)?

---

10   Wæver, O. (2007). Securitization and desecuritization. In B. Buzan, & L. Hansen (Eds.), *International Security* (pp. 66–98). Vol. 3. Widening Security. Los Angeles et al.: SAGE.

11   Baldwin, D. (1997). The concept of security. *Review of International Studies, 23*(1), 5–26.

12   Ullman, R. (1983). Redefining security. *International Security, 8*(1), 129–153.

In recent decades, Critical Security Studies have been addressing these issues, seeking to deepen and broaden the classical state-centric approach and highlighting other aspects of security. Examples include the Copenhagen School, the Paris School, the Welsh School (also known as the Aberystwyth School), and other movements based on social constructivist theory.

Most of the recent work in this respect has been done by Copenhagen School[13] representatives such as Ole Wæver, Barry Buzan and others who, in their writings on securitization theory, rethink several aspects of the traditional perception of the concept of security, and begin to reinterpret and subsequently rigorously analyse it as a speech act. Wæver puts forward and advocates the standpoint that security functions not as a sign transmitted to the communicant, but as an act, an action by means of a statement, analogous to what happens in making a bet, expressing a promise, etc.[14] He relies heavily on J. L. Austin's theory of speech acts.[15]

The foundations of securitization theory have been most comprehensively elucidated in *Security: a new framework for analysis*,[16] the work of Barry Buzan, Ole Wæver and Jaap de Wilde, which combines Buzan's notion of sectoral analysis with the theory of securitization, crucially influenced by Wæver's constructivist view. Notable works of the Copenhagen School include *Understanding Global Security* by Peter Hough[17]; *People, States and Fear* by Barry Buzan[18]; and *The Empire of Security and the Safety of the People* edited by William Bain.[19]

The basic postulate underlying theories similar to the Copenhagen School is social constructivism, which assumes that communication/interaction among members of society plays an active role in the creation, stabilization and transformation of social reality.[20] In this sense, it is important to stress that it is not

---

13   The Copenhagen School is the name given to a group of researchers concentrated at the Conflict and Peace Research Institute (COPRI) in Copenhagen.

14   Wæver, 2007, p. 73.

15   Austin, J. L. (1962). *How to Do Things with Words.* Oxford: Clarendon Press.

16   Buzan, B., Ole Wæver, O., & De Wilde, J. (1998). *Security. A New Framework for Analysis.* Boulder, London: Lynne Rienner Publishers.

17   Hough, P. (2004). *Understanding Global Security.* New York, London: Routledge.

18   Buzan, B. (1991). *People, States and Fear: An Agenda for International Security Studies in the Post-Cold War Era*, 2nd edn. London: Harvester Wheatsheaf.

19   Bain, W. (Ed.) (2006). *The Empire of Security and the Safety of the People.* New York, London: Routledge.

20   Berger, P., & Luckmann, T. (1966). *The Social Construction of Reality: A Treatise in the Sociology of Knowledge.* Garden City, NY: Anchor Books.

essentially a matter of establishing whether something is legitimately considered a security threat, but of establishing what is modelled/constructed as a security threat in speech acts, in the spirit of social constructivism. It is important to point out that for Buzan, Wæver and de Wilde "The defining criterion of security is textual: a specific rhetorical structure that has to be located in discourse."[21]

The Copenhagen School, which perceives security as a speech act but also as an intersubjective process, tends to lean towards those speech acts which have aroused considerable criticism. Some claim that the concept insufficiently explains the relationship between the social environment that must recognize the instance of securitization and the linguistic sharing that presents it (i.e., in Austin's terminology, between illocutionary and perlocutionary acts), and that the original Copenhagen School concept does not provide a developed definition of how the three categories of speech acts are related to the idea of securitization.

Austin described three kinds of speech acts – illocutionary, locutionary and perlocutionary. A locutionary act is "uttering a certain sentence with a certain sense and reference, which again is roughly equivalent to 'meaning' in the traditional sense."[22] When identifying an illocutionary act, we consider the realization of a certain communicative intention ("informing, ordering, warning, undertaking i.e."); they are "utterances which have a certain (conventional) force."[23] It is only the perlocutionary act that is associated with a certain effect: "what we bring about or achieve by saying something, such as convincing, persuading, deterring, and even, say, surprising or misleading."[24] Critics reproach Copenhagen School theorists for not clearly explaining whether to focus on illocutionary or perlocutionary acts in the analysis of securitization. Holger Stritzel points out that the greater the role attributed to the illocution itself, the less relevant its effect on the audience for the analysis of securitization. In contrast, if we emphasize the importance of the audience's acceptance of the speech act, we attribute a greater role to perlocution, which contradicts the original premise in which security is presented as a speech act rather than its perlocutionary consequence.[25]

---

21   Buzan, Wæver, & De Wilde, 1998, p. 176
22   Austin, 1962, p. 108.
23   Austin, 1962, p. 108.
24   Austin, 1962, p. 108.
25   Stritzel, H. (2014). *Security in Translation Securitization Theory and the Localization of Threat*. Basingstoke: Palgrave Macmillan.

We understand these reservations, but we do not see them as an obstacle to the logic of our research on the speech acts of the securitization of Slovak public discourse, since we are more inclined to the view that the locutionary, illocutionary and perlocutionary acts do not represent three acts that are realized one by one by the expedient, but different aspects of the same speech[26]; after all, Austin himself[27] says "the total speech act situation" is the union of three types of speech acts: the locutionary act (the "communicative performance" itself, the utterance), the illocutionary act (expressing the speaker's relation to the utterance), and the perlocutionary act (expressing the elicited effect of the illocutionary act). Following this link (unity of components), we will also carry out our linguistic (primarily lexical) analysis of extracted speech acts in a comprehensive manner. We will also bear in mind the opinion of Stritzel deriving from the Copenhagen School theory concerning the nature of securitizing speech acts, which, according to him, have a strict rhetorical structure: "(a) a generic claim: something is dangerous/an existential threat; (b) a generic warning: if something is not done, the danger/threat will be realized; (c) a generic demand: something should be done; and (d) propositional content: proof and/or reasons are provided to support the claim/warning."[28] For each of these components, however, we will be primarily concerned with the linguistic devices that are used and the intentions behind their use.

Apart from the insufficient explanation of whether to focus on illocutionary or perlocutionary acts in the analysis of securitization, and the absence of clear criteria for measuring the success of securitization steps (which, however, is not essential in terms of the linguistic focus of our research), the criticism of the "post-Copenhagen" generation of securitization theorists is mainly based on the fact that the framework of the Copenhagen School does not provide analytical tools for the conceptual identification of securitizing actors. They are also blamed for allegedly over-emphasizing speech acts at the expense of non-discursive forms of securitization,[29] weak elaboration of the concept of desecuritization,[30] ignoring

---

26   Helbig, G. (1990). *Entwicklung der Sprachwissenschaft seit 1970*. Opladen: Der Westdeutsche Verlag, p. 185.

27   Austin, 1962, p. 147.

28   Stritzel, 2014, p. 48.

29   McDonald, M. (2008). Securitization and the construction of security. *European Journal of International Relations, 14*(4), 563–587.

30   Aradau, C. (2004). Security and the democratic scene: Desecuritization and emancipation. *Journal of International Relations and Development, 7*, 388–413.

the visual dimension of discourse,[31] and limited reflection on the meaning of the social field, context and timing.[32]

Thierry Balzacq (one of the sociologically oriented authors of the so-called Paris School) is a consistent critic, but also a follower and "refiner" of the Copenhagen School's theory of securitization, reproaching it for excessive emphasis on the illocutionary dimension of the speech act, which, according to him, leads to neglecting the role of the audience, over-emphasizing the text, and failing to register the influence of the context on the securitization motion.[33] This, however, is the opinion of a sociologist. Yet, the "over-emphasis on the text" is fully in line with the intentions of our linguistic investigation, and therefore, even with an awareness of the possible legitimacy of the aforementioned "reproaches," in the following research, we will rely on the concept of the Copenhagen School both theoretically and terminologically as a "research design".[34]

1.2 Basic concepts of securitization theory

The basic concepts of the Copenhagen School's theory of securitization include *securitization, referent objects, securitizing actors, functional actors* and *desecuritization.*

---

31   Hansen, L. (2011). Theorizing the image for security studies: Visual securitization and the Muhammad Cartoon Crisis. *European Journal of International Relations, 17*(1), 51–74.

32   Balzacq, T. (2005). The three faces of securitization: Political agency, audience and context. *European Journal of International Relations, 11*(2), 171–201. Balzacq, T. (2011). A theory of securitisation: Origins, core assumptions and variants. Securitization theory. In T. Balzacq (Ed.), *Securitization Theory. How Security Problems Amerge and Dissolve* (pp. 1–30). Milton Park, Abingdon, Oxon: Routledge.

33   Balzacq, 2011, p. 23.

34   This expression used by Petr Martinovsky seemed to us to be apt in respect of the ways and extent of the application of Copenhagen School theories in the present politolinguistic research of Slovak public discourse. In subchapter *Securitization as research design,* it is stated that "the perception of securitization as a research design is linked to the Copenhagen School collective's pivotal and much-cited book *Security – A New Framework for Analysis.* This book not only approaches securitization as a theory, but in many places it recommends specific approaches or illustrates possible applications in empirical research." See Martinovský, P. (2016). *Environmentální bezpečnost v České republice.* Brno: Masarykova univerzita, p. 61.

Securitization represents an intersubjective determination of an existential threat with sufficient salience to exert substantial political effects.[35] It can be regarded as a more radical version of politicization, since the step by which politics moves beyond the established rules of the game, and which frames certain topics either as a special kind of politics or as a matter standing "above" standard political action, is precisely the notion of "security". In terms of theory, any public issue can be placed on a scale ranging from depoliticized [...] to politicized [....] to securitized (the issue is perceived as an existential threat that requires extraordinary measures and justifies action that exceeds the standard boundaries of political procedures).[36]

Referent objects are "things that are seen to be existentially threatened and that have a legitimate claim to survival [...]. The referent object for security has traditionally been the state and, in a more hidden way the nation. [...] But if one follows the securitization approach outlined earlier, a much more open spectrum of possibilities has to be allowed. In principle, securitizing actors can attempt to construct anything as a referent object."[37] It can be the whole of humankind, the biosphere, the state, the economy of a country, the environment, ethnic groups, religion, democratic values of a society, family values or the identity of a particular social group. Whereby the security act is carried out predominantly in the name of a certain collective body and with reference to its situation. "The referent object is that to which one can point and say: 'It has to survive; therefore, it is necessary to ...' "[38]

The reference objects that are presented as the "most threatened" in Slovakia nowadays will be discussed in detail in the following subchapter.

A securitizing actor is typically a person, but it can also be a group, party or institution[39] that performs a security speech act, i.e., declares referent objects to be existentially threatened and sets in motion the process of securitization.[40] This role is traditionally assumed by political leaders, bureaucratic apparatuses,

---

35   Buzan, B., Ole Wæver, O., & De Wilde, J. (1998). *Security. A New Framework for Analysis*. Boulder, London: Lynne Rienner Publishers, p. 25.

36   Buzan, Wæver, & De Wilde, 1998, p. 23–24.

37   Buzan, Wæver, & De Wilde, 1998, p. 36.

38   Buzan, Wæver, & De Wilde, 1998, p. 36.

39   "In the case of a state, the government will usually be the securitizing actor. A government will often be tempted to use security arguments (in relation to the state) when its concern is actually that the government itself is threatened" (Buzan, Wæver, & De Wilde, p. 146.).

40   Buzan, Wæver, & De Wilde, 1998, pp. 35–36.

governments or lobby and pressure groups who argue that it is necessary to ensure the security of the state, nation, civilization or some other collective body, principle, or system.[41] The securitizing actor who presents the threat as objectively existing for a particular referent object thus extracts the topic from the ordinary political process and moves it to the plane of securitization (through the speech act).

While the actors of securitization are mostly politicians, they can also operate outside political circles.[42] such as individuals with considerable social influence (whether in an international or area-specific context).

One of the important variables of social influence is the ability to persuade. In the context of our research, the guiding view of experts is that they perceive the ability to persuade a broad audience as the extent to which an individual is motivated and successful in influencing people who initially disagree with him/her. The process of persuasion involves personality traits (dedication, clarity, trustworthiness, credit, credibility, expertise, integrity) along with the intensity with which the opinion is asserted.[43]

The Slovak securitizing actors, whose speech acts will be subject to our analysis, demonstrate the above-mentioned characteristics, especially the extraordinary dedication and intensity with which they promote their views (mainly in the media and social networks). The degree of their integrity, as well as their trustworthiness, credit and credibility are relative, because they apply only to a certain (albeit significant) part of Slovak society. Today, given the post-factual nature of our time, expertise is also becoming a relative concept. It is enough to declare oneself an expert, or to rely on the opinions of other experts (since the widespread practice of social networks today is literally the viral dissemination of "expert opinions" without indicating specific primary sources). "A large volume of fake news and disinformation is now appearing, especially in the online space. The World Economic Forum has pointed out that fake news and disinformation are currently among the primary dangers to society. Disinformation Facebook pages have several times more interactions than Facebook pages of state institutions."[44] In Slovakia, according to our observations and those of others,

---

41   Buzan, Wæver, & De Wilde, 1998, p. 40.
42   Buzan, Wæver, & De Wilde, 1998, p. 34.
43   Nowak, A., Szamrej, J., & Latané, B. (1990). From private attitude to public opinion: A dynamic theory of social impact. *Psychological Review, 97*(3), 362–376.
44   Višňovský, J., & Prašovská, P. (2022) Pandémia falošných správ v čase pandémie covidu-19 alebo ktorým falošným správam a hoaxom veríme. In A. Sámelová, M. Stanková, & J. Hacek (Eds.), *Fenomén 2022: Médiá a kríza autorít* (pp. 93–107). Bratislava: Univerzita Komenského v Bratislave, p. 95.

this is true to a hypertrophied extent. The topic of "expertise" and disinformation on Slovak Facebook is dealt with in detail by media specialist Vladimír Šnídl, who observes that "several times more Slovaks log in to the virtual space of Facebook at least once a day than watch the news on any television channel in the evening. "The Facebook newsfeed has become for many people what TV news or news websites were just a decade ago."[45] This condition doubtless helps the securitizing actors today in the literally uncontrollable spread of "threats". Their predecessors could not have dreamt of such unlimited opportunities to communicate with potential voters.

The criterion of comprehensibility is fulfilled to the maximum degree possible by the Slovak securitizing actors; their speech acts are sophisticated in terms of the choice of linguistic means; they are as close as possible to the linguistic traditions and (stylistically mostly colloquial) linguistic culture of their target audience; and it is this aspect that will be one of the fundamental vectors of our analysis. An essential point in determining the "persuasiveness rate" of these actors includes their success in influencing people who initially disagreed with them. Although the assessment of this aspect is in the competence of sociologists and political scientists, it is clear from the significant increase in the pre-election preferences (2023) of the securitizing actors of the Slovak political scene that they are also succeeding in influencing a significant number of citizens who initially disagreed with them (or who were not previously interested in their views).

After all, one of the main prerequisites for the success of a securitizing speech act is seen even by representatives of the Copenhagen School in the "social capital of the enunciator, the securitizing actor, who must be in a position of authority, although this should not be defined as official authority [...] the social conditions regarding the position of authority for the securitizing actor – that is, the relationship between speaker and audience and thereby the likelihood of the audience accepting the claims made in a securitizing attempt."[46]

Social networks, as the main contemporary vehicle for disseminating views, provide securitizing actors with an "informational advantage" that their predecessors did not have at the beginning of the 21st century. "A big role is played by the so-called social bubbles, which is a phenomenon that started to be talked about in connection with the advent of social networks. An average Facebook user's friends are people from similar backgrounds with the same

---

45   Šnídl, V. (2017). *Pravda a lož na Facebooku*. Bratislava: N Press s.r.o., p. 8.
46   Buzan, Wæver, & De Wilde, 1998, p. 33.

worldview."[47] This concerns the numerous followers of the Facebook accounts of political figures, parties and other securitizing actors. They uncritically and unconditionally identify with every idea of their "ideological leader" and immediately and actively spread them further in their own communities, whose members share many of the same views. As a result, the articulation of fabricated threats begins to go literally viral. Therefore, at this point we want to highlight the change brought about by the development of Internet technology, and specifically the dominant role of social networks in the process of disseminating threats by specific securitizing actors. This changes the perspective on the way in which the Copenhagen School articulates the role of the public in securitization processes. Today, the public is mainly comprised of the followers of the social media pages of securitizing actors. And since this "new age" public is exceptionally engaged in disseminating posts and writing commentaries (supporting and interpreting in their own way the presented threats), it is no longer just a passive audience; it plays a significant role in the securitization process.

Functional actors affect the dynamics of security relations in the securitized sector. They significantly influence political decisions, yet they do not directly indicate the need for security actions in relation to the referent object.[48] The determination of the threat is an intersubjective, opinion-based delimitation of the elite that has been able to convince others of the urgency of the threat. As a functional actor, the media, for example, are also an effective partner in defining and assessing the threat. The subject, which has the ability to influence them in some way, can also significantly influence the development of the situation.[49] It is the media and social networks that have become the most influential functional actors in recent years, as "never in the past has a person had such a supply of information as in the era of online media. The Internet and social networks spew crises of all kinds at users almost continuously, and the algorithms of the semantic web then display them in prominent places where they cannot be accidentally overlooked. The media have thus become one of the mediators, hence the propagators, of crises. However, it turns out that in many respects the media are also the direct or indirect originators of crises and accelerators of their settling in the minds of the public"[50] Thus, today, the media are the main functional

---

47 Šnídl, 2017.
48 Buzan, Wæver, & De Wilde, 1998, p. 36.
49 Buzan, Wæver, & De Wilde, 1998, p. 124.
50 Sámelová, A. (2022). Fenomén 2022: Médiá a kríza autorít. In A. Sámelová, M. Stanková, & J. Hacek (Eds.), *Fenomén 2022: Médiá a kríza autorít* (pp. 6–8). Bratislava: Univerzita Komenského v Bratislave.

actor facilitating the process of securitization, as they "contribute substantially to the construction of social reality. Part of this reality are the meanings valid in a given discourse and the values applicable in a given ideology."[51] Speaking of "facilitation", we are primarily referring to the prioritization of certain events and actors over others according to certain criteria (i.e., agenda-setting), which is an established journalistic editorial practice. In this context, we can also mention the placement of articles on the newspaper's print or web pages, the arrangement of news in sequence, the prominent and unmissable "sensational" headlines, the size, nature and number of images, etc. "The media choose what to report and how to report it [...] the media, by which we mean managing editors, editors, or the journalists themselves, sort the news by selecting it; they also select the agenda of the topics that come into the recipient's view, giving the impression that they are the most important."[52]

As long as the securitizing actor manages to avoid otherwise binding rules and procedures by asserting the priority and urgency of the existential threat, we are witnessing a successful instance of securitization.[53]

It is important to understand, however, that an actor's securitizing behaviour is not the only guarantee of a successful securitization. Successful securitization is conditional on public acceptance. "A discourse that takes the form of presenting something as an existential threat to a referent object does not by itself create securitization – this is a securitizing move, but the issue is securitized only if and when the audience accepts it as such."[54]

A very important role in the securitization process is played by the actor, whose influence and position in a given society is usually not insignificant. It is also thanks to the actor's influence that a threat becomes a threat, just by the fact that the actor perceives it as such and declares it publicly. In this respect, it should be kept in mind that "government information policy largely influences the implementation of information and communication technology, can create differences in the status of certain types of actors in the form of advantages and disadvantages in relation to information and its use, determines the parameters of government information activities, and significantly affects the political, social, and economic conditions of working with information."[55] The benefitting

---

51 Burton, G., & Jirák, J. (2001). *Úvod do studia medii*. Brno: Barrister & Principal.
52 Burton, & Jirák, 2011, p. 240
53 Buzan, Wæver, & De Wilde, 1998, p. 26.
54 Buzan, Wæver, & De Wilde, 1998, p. 25.
55 Šušol et al. (2012). *Informačná politika*. 2. vydanie. Bratislava: STIMUL.

securitizing actor therefore has an incomparably greater potential for fulfilling their intentions (the securitization can only be considered accomplished if it is also successful in relation to the recipients who accept it). Subsequently, based on society's consent and support, the actor can take extraordinary measures or circumvent the rules and laws (legitimize the breaking of rules).

What also matters are the characteristics of the reported threats, which either facilitate securitization or, on the contrary, make it more difficult,[56] as well as the linguistic means of its implementation.

Concerning the characteristics of the reported threats, in the process of the analysis we will take into account, among other things, the opinions of experts on the peculiarities of people's perception of the threats and risks presented to them. Bruce Schneier provides a remarkable table entitled *Conventional Wisdom About People and Risk Perception* in which he states, among other things, that we exaggerate risks that are: personified / often talked about / beyond our control or externally imposed / intentional, man-made / related to our children / morally offensive / not like our current situation.[57]

In our view, these criteria are directly correlated with the discourse strategies of the securitization process, and experienced securitizing actors undoubtedly keep them in mind.

As for the linguistic means used in securitizing speech acts, we believe that the use of expressive, emotionally-coloured expressions, constant metaphorization, hyperbolization, infiltration of substandard lexis (sociolectisms, jargonisms, argot, vulgarisms) must have a significant persuasive effect. Complemented by the continuous media presentation of horrific images of war, terrorist acts, refugees, natural cataclysms, various manifestations of the growing economic crisis (rising prices, etc.), they spread fear twice as fast, which no doubt contributes to the successful securitization of the current key topics – migration, the economic crisis, inflation, rising poverty, refusal of aid to Ukraine, questioning of our membership in the EU, NATO. It is successful because the media and social networks (as functional actors) and the securitizing actors (mostly right-wing extremists and left-wing populists) continuously link these themes through a strong verbal and visual presence.

Once the "danger" is removed, there is a stage of desecuritization in which previously securitized issues cease to be perceived as a potential threat by society

---

56   Buzan, Wæver, & De Wilde, 1998, p. 33.
57   Schneier, B. (2008). The psychology of security. In S. Vaudenay (Ed.), *AFRICACRYPT 2008, LNCS 5023* (pp. 50–79). Heidelberg: Springer-Verlag.

and are once again regulated by the normal rules. The ultimate goal then, is not to achieve real objective security, but to remove the issue from the category of securitized dangers, from discursive practice.

This usually happens after elections, when the securitization goals are achieved and the previous manipulation of voters by articulating "threats" has already gained its political effect. For example, in 2016 in Slovakia, the continuous demonization of migrants (migrants as a threat to the Slovak economy, to the social sphere, to the cultural and religious identity of Slovaks, etc.) was the main pre-election theme of the *SMER* party. However, it was forgotten as irrelevant after their victory (after the completion of successful securitization) and formation of the government, because migrants have never posed a real threat to Slovakia[58] and the topic of "dangerous migrants" had already fulfilled its securitization "pre-election" purpose. The process of desecuritization had taken place, and other pressing social issues (problems of healthcare, education, social security, corruption) rose to the fore.

Proponents of securitization theory have been blamed by critics for failing to analyse how securitization, through speech acts, becomes intersubjective and restructures social relations. In the "textual" view of securitization as a socially productive speech act that justifies the decisions of politicians to introduce "urgent measures", a different, "contextual" interpretation can also be found in the works of securitization theorists, based on the singling out of factors facilitating securitization.[59] In addition to the particular attributes of the speech act that allow it to be perceived as a securitization practice, the very specifics of the assumed threat also influence its success (certain situations are much easier to present as a danger compared to others). Moreover, the authority of the actor in the eyes of the recipient also contributes to the success of the act of securitization. However, several critics of the theory point out that if the "textual" and "contextual" understanding of securitization are not to contradict each other, then it must begin to be seen not as a separate speech act ascribing one and the same fixed meaning to reality, but as a process of meaning creation itself, anchored deeply in a discursive context that transforms an individual proposition into a collective dominant narrative.[60]

---

58   Slovakia has the third lowest share of foreigners among the countries of the European Union as of 31.12.2022, detailed data can be found at International Organization for Migration, Slovakia (2022, December 31). *Migrácia na Slovensku*. https://www.iom. sk/sk/migracia/migracia-na-slovensku.html

59   Buzan, Wæver, & De Wilde, 1998, p. 33.

60   Stritzel, H. (2007). Towards a theory of securitization: Copenhagen and beyond. *European Journal of International Relations, 13*(3), 357–383, p. 369.

1.3 Key referent objects (threatened entities) in the securitization process in Slovakia

Reflecting on the dynamic transformation period of the 1990s in Europe, and on the disintegration of the former Eastern bloc, Copenhagen School researchers point to a range of political and social processes such as globalization, migration flows, cultural imperialism, as widely manifested in political and media discourse as a potential threat to "public security", i.e., the ability of a society to retain its essential characteristics despite changing conditions and potential or existing threats.[61]

International relations theorists who failed to foresee the end of the Cold War and the disintegration of the bipolar system had to adapt their conceptual apparatus to the processes that resulted from these changes.[62] The subject matter expanded and at the same time began to " fragment" into " partial" concepts of security that emerged in the 1990s: personal security (of individuals), gender security, economic security, collective security, food security, ecological security, etc.[63] In the pan-European context, the themes of economic stability, increasing energy dependence, ecology, global epidemics, global warming, international terrorism, geopolitical conflicts close to European borders, frozen and active conflicts in the post-Soviet region, the events of the Arab Spring, migration problems, have been successfully articulated as threats[64] and they are being securitized as a possible cause of the danger of terrorism and the loss of the cultural identity of Europeans.

In recent years, Slovakia has witnessed a growth of nationalism (at times even with traits of neo-Nazism), Euroscepticism, extremism, political and cultural Russophilia. Representatives and advocates of these ideologies and views, and numerous securitizing actors posing as the main threatened entities (reference objects) advocate the economic security of Slovakia, the social security of Slovaks, food security, traditional family values, traditional Christian values, Slovak cultural identity and more broadly the "historical Slavic unity". Next, we will focus on speech acts articulating the aforementioned threats, highlighting

---

61 Buzan, B., & Hansen, L. (2009). *The Evolution of International Security Studies.* Cambridge: Cambridge University Press, p. 84.

62 Buzan, Hansen, 2009, p. 187.

63 Buzan, Hansen, 2009, pp. 136–141.

64 Lidák, J. (2014). International migration, Europe and migration from Africa. *Asian and African Studies, 23*(2), 226–254.

(graphically) and then analysing the linguistic means used most frequently in the process of the "pre-election" intimidation of Slovaks.

The activities of the national-conservative and nationalist movement *Republika*, are a notable example of successful securitization (of the aforementioned "threatened entities") on the Slovak political scene. In less than 2 years of existence, it reached an electoral preference of 8.7 % in July 2023 (according to Focus Agency polls).[65] Successful securitization is also demonstrated by the fact that they managed to collect 45 797 signatures for the 2022 referendum for early elections, and to co-organize the mass "Slovak March for Peace" (3 March 2023), primarily intended as a demonstration against EU and NATO policy and the government's support for Ukraine, and which "also featured banners with the letter "Z", *Stop EU and NATO* and *I will never take up a gun against Russia*".[66]

This political success is mainly due to their extraordinary activity on social networks (which in this respect makes them a significant functional securitizing actor), where they demonize the current political, social and economic events in Slovakia and evoke a sense of threat to the very livelihood of the "decent" citizens of Slovakia. In the article *The twin of Smer is growing. Republika is sweeping social networks, reaching out to the young and wants a government with Fico and Danko* in the *Postoj* newspaper (10 May 2023)[67] Juraj Brezáni observed that "an April poll by the Focus agency measured the *Republika* movement of MEP Milan Uhrík, Kotleba's former right-hand man, at almost 10 %, which has led the head of *Republika* to claim that it is the strongest pro-national party in the country [...] Almost 40 % of the *Republika's* voters are between 35 and 54 years of age and up to 36 % of the voters are under 34 years of age, making *Republika* the second most popular political party among young people after *Progresívne Slovensko* (Progressive Slovakia). The fact that *Republika* manages to appeal to them is related to the movement's strong activity on social networks. In the top five most influential political accounts on Facebook there are three

65 Tlačová agentúra Slovenskej republiky, TASR (2023, July 28). Prieskum: Matovičova koalícia by do parlamentu neprešla, SNS aj SaS tesne áno. *Sme*. https://domov.sme.sk/c/23199219/prieskum-politickych-stran-jul-focus-2023.html

66 Dugovič, T. (2023, March 3). Na Pochod za mier do Bratislavy prišli tisíce ľudí. Protestovalo sa skôr proti NATO ako proti Rusku. *Štandard*. https://standard.sk/327 392/v-bratislave-sa-kona-pochod-za-mier-demonstranti-su-na-hviezdoslavovom-namesti-prislo-niekolko-tisic-ludi-akcia-je-pokojna

67 Brezáni, J. (2023, May 23). Dvojička Smeru rastie. Republika valcuje sociálne siete, oslovuje mladých a chce vládu s Ficom a Dankom- *Postoj*. https://www.postoj.sk/130 065/republika-valcuje-socialne-siete-oslovuje-mladych-a-dokonca-aj-liberalov

accounts from *Republika*. This follows from the data provided to *Postoj* by New School Communications. Although Robert Fico, the head of *Smer*, is by far the most influential on the networks, Milan Uhrík, the leader of *Republika* is the second [...] the third most influential political account on Facebook is that of Tomáš Špaček, a member of the movement, and the fifth most influential is that of the deputy chairman of the movement, M. Mazurek". Every day and openly in their posts they share the Kremlin narrative according to which the global evil and the cause of all international crises and conflicts are solely NATO, the US, Brussels, Soros, NGOs and liberals. They are also presented as the main threats to Slovakia.

On their official website[68] they propose a program which, from the linguistic (stylistic) point of view, does not correspond with the genre of the official party program statement, as in an attempt to get closer to the addressees and to manipulate their emotions, they also use stylistically marked, colloquial, emotionally-coloured lexis. What we see here is not primarily an informative, communicative function, but a persuasive function that determines the composition and the resulting style of the text. Instead of the expected prevalence of lexis based on direct denomination (one of the main lexical features of the official style), information (alluding to imminent danger) is also processed indirectly through metaphorical imagery, the metonymic principle, or the use of tropes, figures of speech and phraseological devices. The document does not correspond to the genre of an official (constructive) party program even in terms of content, but it evokes the feeling of threat to all components of social and political life in the Slovak Republic from the existing government, and in this regard, it is significant for the topic of our research. All of the following examples come from the program mentioned above, and are illustrative of the entities (referent objects) that are most often thematized as endangered in Slovakia today, and the "popularly comprehensible" linguistic means (including ideological clichés and platitudes from the so-called alternative media) that are used in doing so:

– **traditional Slovak family**:

SL → *vytvorenie podmienok pre zvýšenie pôrodnosti* **slušných rodín** / *ochrana slovenských rodín pred* **nebezpečnými ideológiami**[69]

---

68   Republika (2023, September). *Program*. https://www.hnutie-republika.sk/program/
69   EL → the creation of conditions for increasing the birth rate of **decent families** / protection of Slovak families from **dangerous ideologies**

- **social certainties:**

  SL → *zabrániť ďalšiemu* **zbedačovaniu poctivých ľudí/** *Slovensko nesmie byť* **otrokáreň!**[70]

- **social justice** which is mainly thematized through the discourse strategy *US* (honest but poor working Slovaks) *versus* THEM (welfare recipients, unadaptable citizens, which is a widespread and readily recognizable Slovak euphemism for Roma citizens):

  SL → *Sociálnu politiku postavíme na princípe spravodlivosti, aby sa viac* **oplatilo pracovať** *ako len* **poberať dávky.** *Občania, ktorí sa* **nechcú prispôsobiť** *nemôžu dostávať zadarmo to, čo si všetci ostatní musia platiť.* Pre **pracujúcu chudobu,** *ktorá sa chce vymaniť zo* **špirály predražených dlhov,** *poskytneme výhodné sociálne úvery / Chceme, aby sa na Slovensku sa slušní a poctiví ľudia mali vždy lepšie ako* **gauneri a zločinci.**[71]

- **sovereignty, territorial integrity of the Slovak Republic and security of citizens:**

  SL → *súčasnú severoatlantickú alianciu NATO považujeme za* **prežitok studenej vojny** *a za* **zdroj vojenského napätia** *a konfliktov vo svete / o* **vystúpení Slovenska z NATO** *môžu rozhodnúť občania v referende. Zásadne* **odmietame rozmiestňovanie cudzích vojsk** *a základní na Slovensku/ história nás poučila, že skutočne spoliehať sa môžeme vždy len sami na seba. A k tomu potrebujeme sebavedomé a silné ozbrojené sily. Pevný železný štít, ktorý bude* **chrániť rodiny a domovy nás všetkých vo dne aj v noci**[72]

- **civil rights, rule of law:**

  SL → *bude vládnuť* **spravodlivosť a férovosť** */ zlepšíme vymožiteľnosť zákonov najmä* **pre bežných občanov** */ Zavedieme* **absolútnu slobodu** *slova a názorov / Prijmeme zákon na prísnu* **kontrolu činnosti politických mimovládnych organizácií,** *a to najmä tých, ktoré sú financované zo zahraničia / Zrušíme minimálne kvórum pre platnosť*

---

70 EL → prevent the further **impoverishment of honest people/** Slovakia must not be **a slave market!**

71 EL → We will base social policy on the principle of fairness, so that it **pays more to work** than to **receive social benefits.** Citizens who **do not want to adapt** cannot get for free what everyone else has to pay for. **For the working poor** who want to escape **the spiral of overpriced debts,** we will provide favourable social loans / We want decent and honest people in Slovakia to always have a better life than **crooks and criminals.**

72 EL → we regard the current NATO as **a relic of the Cold War** and **a source of military tension** and conflict in the world / **Slovakia's exit from NATO** can be decided by the citizens in a referendum. We categorically reject the **deployment of foreign troops and bases** in Slovakia / **history has taught us** that we can only ever truly rely on ourselves. And for that we need a confident and strong military. A solid iron shield **to protect the families and homes of us all, day and night.**

*referenda a výsledok referenda spravíme ústavne záväzným / Pracujeme profesionálne a na úrovni, tak **ako sa sluší a patrí. Žiadna 4.** cenová*[73]

- **nation-state interest:**

SL → *Nechceme žiadnych imigrantov, žiadne pretláčanie **zvrátených ideológií**, žiadnu európsku federalizáciu a žiadne **politické rozkazy z Bruselu** / nechceme byt súčasťou **európskeho žalára národov** pod diktátom progresívneho Bruselu a Washingtonu / chrániť občanov Slovenska **pred škodlivými politickými** vplyvmi zahraničných ambasád, mimovládnych organizácií a globalistických štruktúr / sme pripravení iniciovať referendum o **vystúpení Slovenska z EÚ** / **Odmietame protiruské besnenie** a sankcie a budeme pracovať na zlepšení vzťahov aj so štátmi na východ od nás, vrátane zlepšenia vzťahov s Ruskou federáciou.*[74]

- **distinctive culture and traditions:**

SL → *chceme rozvíjať **zdravé vlastenectvo** / Odmietame kultúrne a mediálne **pretláčanie LGBT agendy a propagáciu drog, potratov a eutanázie.** Nestotožňujeme sa s presadzovaním **ideológie multikulturalizmu a materializmu** / Sme odhodlaní brániť naše národné hodnoty a tradície v **kultúrno-ideologickom zápase s „progresivizmom"** / V duchu nášho **historického dedičstva** vytvoríme Centrum **slovanských kultúr** / obmedzíme množstvo **otravnej reklamy** v televízii a zlepšíme ochranu detí pred **nemravnosťou v médiách** / budeme presadzovať ochranu verejnosti pred **mediálnymi manipuláciami** a preveríme vplyv mimovládnych organizácií financovaných zo zahraničia na kultúrnu a mediálnu scénu / zrušíme názorovú*

---

73   EL → **justice and fairness** will govern / we will improve the enforceability of laws, especially **for ordinary citizens** / we will introduce **absolute freedom** of speech and opinion / we will pass a law to strictly **control the activities of political NGOs**, especially those that are financed from abroad / we will abolish the minimum quorum for a referendum to be valid and make the result of the referendum constitutionally binding / We work professionally and with high standards, **as decent people do. No 4th price group.** (a literal translation of a Slovak phrase which means *a cheap pub of dubious quality for people with dubious reputation*, authors' note).

74   EL → We want no immigrants, no imposition of **perverted ideologies**, no European federalization and no **political orders from Brussels** / we do not want to be part of **the European dungeon of nations** under the dictates of progressive Brussels and Washington / to protect Slovak citizens **from harmful political** influences of foreign embassies, NGOs and globalist structures / we are ready to initiate a referendum on **Slovakia's exit from the EU** / **We reject the anti-Russian rampage** and sanctions and will work to improve relations with countries to the east of Slovakia, including improving relations with the Russian Federation.

cenzúru, zavedieme **absolútnu slobodu slova** *a posilníme právo občanov na slobodný prístup k informáciám či už z masmédií, alebo tzv. alternatívnych médií.*[75]

- **poor regions:**

SL → *investície presmerujeme do najmenej rozvinutých regiónov, aby mali ľudia* **slušné** *živobytie aj tam a* **nemuseli opúšťať rodiny** *kvôli cestovaniu za prácou / Zastavíme* **vyľudňovanie vidieka**[76]

- **traditional agriculture, living environment:**

SL → *Nedovolíme* **skupovanie slovenskej vody a pôdy** *cudzincami a* **používanie GMO** *na území SR. Namiesto toho zjednodušíme predaj z dvora a opäť zlegalizujeme tradičný domáci chov / odmietame rôzne* **nedomyslené (európske) „zelené plány"**, *ktoré nespĺňajú základné odborné kritériá / Zastavíme* **nekontrolované drancovanie** *a vývoz surového dreva zo štátnych lesov do zahraničia.*[77]

- **public healthcare:**

SL → *zabezpečíme* **bezplatnú** *zdravotnú starostlivosť na celom území Slovenska / Skoncujeme s ponižujúcim nosením si* **vlastného toaletného papiera** *a hygienických potrieb do nemocníc. Rozhodovanie v zdravotníctve vymaníme* **spod vplyvu finančných**

---

75 EL → We want to develop **a healthy patriotism** / We reject the cultural and media **propagation of the LGBT agenda and the promotion of drugs, abortion and euthanasia.** We do not identify with the enforcement of **the ideology of multiculturalism and materialism** / We are determined to protect our national values and traditions in **the cultural-ideological struggle with "progressivism"** / In the spirit of our historical heritage, we will create the Centre of **Slavic Cultures** // reduce the amount of annoying advertising on TV and improve the protection of children from **obscenity in the media** / we will promote the protection of the public from **media manipulation** and investigate the influence of foreign-funded NGOs on the cultural and media scene / we will abolish opinion censorship, introduce **absolute freedom of speech** and strengthen the right of citizens to free access to information, whether from the mass media or the so-called alternative media.

76 EL → We will redirect investment to the least developed regions so that people have **a decent living** there too and don't have to **leave their families** to travel to find work / We will stop the **depopulation** of rural areas

77 EL → We will not allow **the buying up of Slovak water and land** by foreigners and **the use of GMOs** on the territory of the Slovak Republic. Instead, we will simplify farmer-to-customer selling and re-legalize traditional domestic farming / We reject the various **ill-conceived (European) "green plans"** that do not meet basic expert criteria / We will stop **the uncontrolled plundering** and export of raw timber from the state forests to foreign countries.

skupín, pochybných mimovládnych organizácií a farmaceutických firiem tak, aby
bol na prvom mieste vždy *záujem pacienta*.[78]

These utopian-looking promises presented as an electoral program are
formulated in a linguistically sophisticated way in relation to the threatened
entities, constructing the "dangers" threatening them in an unqualified and
dehumanizing way, and placing themselves in the position of the only saviours
(from *further impoverishment, slave market, crooks and criminals from NGOs,
LGBT, multiculturalism, progressivism, globalists, liberals*). The rescue of
threatened entities (referent objects) will be carried out *professionally and to a
high standard, as is appropriate. No 4th price group.* The prevailing colloquial,
clichéd expressions, publicisms, colloquial metaphors, slang, expressive lexis,
stigmatizing expressions and colloquial phrasemes, clearly resonate with the
recipient (as reflected in the pre-election preferences). Of course, the tendency
to increase the "colloquiality" of texts with an implicit manipulative intent is not
an "invention" of the representatives of the *Republika* movement, but a general
trend of contemporary communication mediated on the Internet, and in the last
decade it has been noted by several Slovak scholars studying media and public
discourse in the online environment.

"If we focus on the colloquial nature of texts, we find it mainly on the lexical
level. It is manifested in the use of colloquial, non-figurative, but also figurative,
i.e., phraseological devices, paroemias and expressive words, often colloquial
or even non-standard language expressions… The motivated use of non-
standard language is functional, conscious and deliberate, and the frequency
of its occurrence has been increasing"[79]. In our case, the employment of non-
standard language is motivated (in an attempt to increase the persuasive effect
of the text) and deliberate (in an attempt to get "linguistically" closer to the
target audience).

The same traditional rhetorical strategy of populists ONE OF YOU – TO MY
FOLKS (i.e., I think like you – I speak like you, your linguistic means are mine
too) is used by the leading representatives of the *Republika* movement on their
highly popular Facebook accounts as well, thus manipulating their audience on the

---

78   EL → We will provide **free healthcare** throughout the territory of Slovakia / We will
     put an end to the humiliating task of bringing your **own toilet paper** and toiletries to
     hospitals. We will liberate healthcare decision-making **from the influence of financial
     groups, dubious NGOs and pharmaceutical companies** so that the **patient's interest**
     always comes first.

79   Jasinská, L. (2019). *Hovorové lexémy v publicistických textoch.* Košice: UPJŠ v Košiciach.

emotional level. By way of illustration, the following are examples of securitization tactics from the Facebook account of the movement's chairman Milan Uhrík[80] (from May 2023) that logically (the format of the social network allows it today) demonstrate an even greater prevalence of non-standard language, slang, taboo and substandard words, as well as striking emotional-expressive lexical stylemes compared to the movement's official program. A similar mode of expression "combined with the overall provocativeness, harshness, aggressiveness and even cynicism of the portrayal of the discussed themes, significantly shifts the boundaries of taste and fundamentally modifies stylistic standards"[81]:

> SL → *Vládni **babráci** priviedli Slovensko do krízy a chaosu. Nefunkčný parlament? Rozbitý štát? Vláda bez mandátu? Máme toho dosť!* **Upraceme tento bordel!** *Poďte voliť!/ nás **Naďovia** ubezpečovali, že vraj tu žiadne americké základne nebudú. Nuž, po voľbách treba Američanom **poďakovať a poslať ich domov** / Keď sa sem **valili imigranti**, vtedy sa hraničné kontroly robiť "nedali". Keď je Globsec, tak zrazu sa dajú. Čaputovej priority v praxi / Uhrík Čaputovej: Už nespite a konajte, Hegerovu **bandu** treba odvolať! / Slovensko **zaplavilo** kontaminované ukrajinské obilie. **Podradné** ukrajinské obilie na Slovensku nechceme! Minister pôdohospodárstva **uchmatol 1,5 milióna eur a zdrhol**. Čo robí Čaputová? Vraj sa vyjadrí až budúci týždeň, **keď sa vyspí**... / Toto umelo vyvolané zdražovanie je ďalším dôkazom nezmyselnosti európskej politiky, ktorá **si sama strieľa do kolena**. **Brusel** Slovákom v podstate odkázal: "**Držte hubu a to toxické obilie z Ukrajiny jedzte!** / Hnutie REPUBLIKA **pretlačilo** cez parlament zákon, ktorý výrazne eliminuje riziko falšovania volieb.*[82]

---

80 Uhrík, Milan (2023). Facebook. https://www.facebook.com/ing.milan.uhrik

81 Horváth, M. (2017). Uvoľnenie štýlových noriem vplyvom postmoderného diskurzu. *Slovenčinár*, 4(1), 9–15.

82 EL → The government **incompetents** have led Slovakia into crisis and chaos. A dysfunctional parliament? A broken state? A government without a mandate? We have had enough of that! **Let's clean up this mess!** Come and vote! / **the Naďs** (plural form of the surname of the former Slovak Minister of Defense, authors' note) assured us that there would be no American bases here. Well, after the elections, we should **thank Americans and send them home** / When the **immigrants were pouring in here**, it was "impossible" to do border controls they said. Now that Globsec is taking place, suddenly it is possible. Čaputová's priorities in practice / Uhrík to Čaputová: Don't sleep. Act, Heger's **gang** must be dismissed! / Slovakia is **flooded** with contaminated Ukrainian grain. We do not want **inferior** Ukrainian grain in Slovakia! The Minister of Agriculture **grabbed 1.5 million euros and ran away**. What is Čaputová doing? Apparently, she will comment next week **when she wakes up**... / This artificially induced increase in prices is another proof of the absurdity of European policy, which **is shooting itself in the foot**. **Brussels** has essentially told Slovaks: **'Shut up and eat that toxic grain from Ukraine!'** / The REPUBLIKA movement **has pushed** a law **through** parliament that significantly eliminates the risk of election fraud.

Milan Mazurek, the deputy chairman, is not far behind the movement's chairman in intimidating Slovaks; the following examples are from the Faceboun account of Milan Mazurek[83] (May 2023). The graphic form of the original, namely the deliberate use of capitals to emphasize the idea, is retained:

> SL → *POZOR! OPÄŤ NÁM sem chcú **natlačiť nelegálnych cudzincov!** BRUSEL pretláča nové kvóty! Liberálne a progresívne strany pokojne Slovensko zaplavia nelegálmi! Hnutie Republika ich s týmito návrhmi **pošle kade ľahšie!** Slovensko si uchránime! / OCHRÁŇME naše DETI pred tými **zvrátenosťami**. Žiadne ideologické **mimovládky a pomätenci** v školách! Chceme, aby mal každý rodič právo neposlať svoje dieťa na **bludárske prednášky úchylákov** a rôznych ideologických mimovládok! / **Nenažrané** obchodné reťazce **prinútime sa uskromniť!** TOTO El Dorado, ktoré majú reťazce na Slovensku, musí skončiť! / VLASTNÉ MÄSO a mlieko, bez pokút a **šikany!** / ZÁKAZ ÁUT so spaľovacími motormi je **dielom bláznov!** Skratka **čisté šialenstvo**, ktoré vo výsledku môže **pripraviť** obrovské množstvá ľudí **o prácu a uvrhnúť do chudoby** veľkú časť Slovenska! /Ak nám vezmú hotovosť, stratíme všetku kontrolu nad svojimi životmi! Republika zavedie právo na hotovosť do Ústavy a ochráni ľudí pred **digitálnou totalitou!**[84]*

Looking at the extracted texts through the lens of Ján Findra's pragmatic classification of stylemes[85] (3 oppositions in relation to the definition of linguistic units, namely 1. unmarkedness – markedness, 2. notionality – emotionnality/expressiveness, and 3. neutrality – stylistic colouring), it becomes clear that markedness, expressiveness, and stylistic colouring are their obvious features. This expert of Slovak stylistics concluded only relatively recently (20 years ago) that "the presence of conspicuous words (e.g., slang) is undesirable in

---

83   Mazurek, M. (2023, May). Facebook. https://www.facebook.com/MilanMazurek. Republika

84   EL → ATTENTION! AGAIN they want **to cram illegal foreigners in here!** BRUSSELS **is pushing through** new quotas! Liberal and progressive parties will quietly **flood Slovakia with illegals!** The Republika Movement will **send them packing** with these proposals! We will protect Slovakia! / LET'S PROTECT OUR CHILDREN from these **perversions**. No more ideological **NGO's and freaks** in schools! We want every parent to have the right not to send their child to **the delusional lectures of perverts** and various ideological NGOs! / We will force the **rapacious** supermarket chains **to cut back!** THIS **El Dorado** that the chains have in Slovakia has to stop! / OUR OWN MEAT and MILK, without fines and **bullying!** / BANNING combustion engine cars is **the work of fools!** In short, **pure madness,** which in the end can **put** huge numbers of people **out of work and plunge** a large part of Slovakia **into poverty!** / If they take our cash, we lose all control over our lives! Republika will introduce the right to cash into the Constitution and protect people from **digital totalitarianism!**

85   Findra, J. (2004). *Štylistika slovenčiny*. Martin: Osveta.

communication instances of a public or official nature. The entry of expressive words into similar texts is usually felt as a certain distortion or even deformation of standard expression practices."[86] However, securitizing actors operating on social networks today are fundamentally changing the notion of the standards of "communication instances of a public nature". Expressive lexical units *(incompetents, mess, shut up, send packing, delusional lectures of perverts, rapacious chains)* are the basis of their communication, a manner of simplistic presentation of threats, because emotionality is inherently linked with expressiveness, and emotionality is a prerequisite for the successful manipulation of the recipient. Expressive linguistic devices add variety to the communication and contribute to the deliberate formation of attitudes and opinions of the recipients. Thus, in public discourse, through the formation of "new linguistic traditions" in the online communication sphere (media, social networks), both stylistic and communicative standards are gradually being modified.

In recent years, leading Slovak linguist Juraj Dolník has also repeatedly drawn attention to this negative phenomenon, namely "the tendency toward the de-intellectualization of linguistic communication, to its simplification, leading to easy comprehensibility, so that communication is easily accessible to the widest possible range of recipients. This tendency towards the democratization of linguistic communication by reducing its recipient complexity is consistent with consumer-cultural comfort, contributes to the stifling of spiritual activities and reinforces the inclination to persist in superficial mental processing of stimuli".[87] However, as can be seen from the above examples, the actors of securitization in Slovakia are far removed from such "noble" considerations. They fully adapt their speech acts both lexically and stylistically to the "recipient insistence" of their audience and to the peculiarities of their "spiritual activities".

The outcome of the Slovak securitization discourse, which views various societal phenomena as potential threats to diverse referent objects, is, among other things, the shifting of meaning (resemantization) of individual denominations that have traditionally been used.[88] For example, the meaning

---

86   Findra, 2004, p. 25.

87   Dolník, J. (2020). Komunikačná kultúra. *Slovenská reč*, 1, 8–27.

88   This process is, of course, characteristic not only for Slovak securitization discourse but also for the securitization discourses of other areas. In Germany, for instance, the term "Gastarbeiter" (invited worker) carried a neutral to positive connotation in the 1960s, but nowadays it is a pejorative term for economic migrants. It has even spread to other linguistic areas, such as Russia, where it is used as a derogatory, dysphemistic label for cheap labour from the former Soviet republics.

of the originally neutral unit "migrant" shifted from neutral to negative in the context of the extremely negatively-charged securitization debate instigated by SMER party representatives prior to the 2016 Slovak parliamentary elections.

Significantly, the same "threat" was raised again, as one of the pre-election topics for 2023, by the same securitizing actors (the leading figures of the SMER party[89]): *It was Robert Fico who **slashed** (literal meaning of the original Slovak expression: brutally slit, authors' note) **the EU's migration quotas** – no fine talk, but straightforward action. We reject **the migration pact** and we have confirmed it a hundred times. We have always been leaders in the opposition to migration… We **have always protected Slovakia** and we always will. From **the unregulated migration** as well as from American soldiers[90] / In Michalovce and in Trebišov (towns in eastern Slovakia, authors' note) **people are having** problems with Ukrainians; for several months they have been coming across the border **to plunder cash** from ATMs because they **speculated with the exchange rate** – and Slovaks couldn't get the cash. In the shops, Slovaks have half-empty trolleys because they no longer have money for overpriced food, but **Ukrainians' trolleys are** full, **bursting at the seams.** The government only focuses on helping Ukrainians who **ride around in Bavarians** (literal translation of the Slovak colloquial expression for BMWs, authors' note) and **don't give a damn about Slovaks.**[91]*

Thus, one of the new meanings of the term "migrant" is now associated with "security threat". While a few years ago referred to a person who, for various reasons (economic, political, social), left their country of origin and settled in the country of destination, currently, in addition to its previous connotations (a person of another culture, a foreigner, an Arab, a Muslim, a Ukrainian, a black person), it has acquired a new meaning, mainly related to competition on the labour market, with a negative image of a social group dependent on state aid (in the current Slovak linguistic representation of the world, it is mostly the linguistic cliché "they live off our taxes"), with security in terms of the alleged increase in crime (which does not have to be confirmed statistically, even an isolated case with great resonance in the media or social networks is sufficient), or

---

89   Except for the 20-month term of Iveta Radičová's government (2010–2012) the SMER-SD party ruled in Slovakia in various coalition combinations from 2006 to 2020, in 2020–2023 SMER-SD was in the opposition, and in July 2023, according to data from the Focus agency, it had the highest electoral preferences. Source: Focus (2023, July 28). Volebný prieskum agentúry Focus. *Sme.* https://volby.sme.sk/pref/1/politicke-str any/p/focus/2023-07-28

90   Blaha, Ľ. (2023, April 26). Telegram. https://t.me/s/LubosBlahaSmer

91   Blaha, Ľ. (2023, April 28). Telegram. https://t.me/s/LubosBlahaSmer

with the threat to the indigenous society in terms of the preservation of cultural traditions. Even terms that previously seemed to be meaning-neutral (liberalism, multiculturalism, NGOs, progressivism) are subject to resemantization in the process of securitization, as evidenced both by the above examples from the social networks of the *Republika* movement and by our research presented in the following chapters.

1.4 Securitization from the perspective of discourse analysis

To uncover the rules of how securitization operates, it is methodologically helpful to follow the procedures of discourse analysis. We can start from the three-dimensional model proposed by Norman Fairclough.[92] The first level is textual, where the focus is on the linguistic analysis of the discourse fragments forming the research corpus. The second dimension is discursive practice, which covers issues of the production, distribution and consumption of texts and the detection of different types of discourse depending on social factors (it is assumed that texts are specifically produced in specific social contexts, specifically disseminated and consumed). The third dimension covers social practice, where the focus is on whether discourse practice reproduces or restructures existing discourse arrangements and its concrete consequences in society.[93]

The relevant premises for discourse analysis offer a model based on a combination of David Baldwin's conceptualizing questions: Whose security? Security for which values? Security/protection from what? and the so-called vertical and horizontal axes of the Copenhagen School. This provides a clear theoretical framework for the easier identification of referent objects (in answer to the first question) and the source of threats (in answer to the third question). It is a scale on which, in principle, any public topic can be placed. A topic can be depoliticized, politicized or securitized (which can be perceived as a more radical form of politicization). It is to some extent a subjective process of highlighting a particular issue, which thus comes to be understood as an existential threat, demands extraordinary measures and justifies actions that go beyond the standard boundaries of political procedures.[94]

---

92 Fairclough, N. (1996). A reply to Henry Widdowson's "Discourse analysis: A critical view". *Language & Literature*, 5(1), pp. 49–56.

93 Cingerová, N. (2012). Štruktúrovanie diskurzu v teórii E. Laclaua a Ch. Mouffovej a jej miesto v rámci diskurzných štúdií. *Jazyk a kultúra*, 9, pp. 1–7.

94 Buzan, B., & Wæver O. (2003). *Regions and Powers: The Structure of International Security*. Cambridge: Cambridge University Press, p. 71.

The referent objects (international system, regional system, state, national community, human beings) are on the vertical axis and thus their qualitative change is captured. In addition to the state, intangible entities, such as human rights or democratic principles, can also become referent objects. The sources of threats constitute the horizontal axis. The Copenhagen School divides them into five sectors: military, political, societal, economic and environmental.

The term societal security was first used by Barry Buzan in his book *People, States and Fear*,[95] in which he argues that the relationship between security and the identity of different groups (especially in the context of Europe) is an important element of the stability and security of the state, which he refers to as societal security. This concept explained the conflicts between the state and different societal groups existing in the state. "Only rarely are state and societal boundaries coterminous. This provides a first motive for taking societal security seriously."[96]

The question "security of what values?" is not explicitly captured in the model, but the Copenhagen School representatives address it in their work in the sense that individuals and different social groups may have different values, even different value priorities, such as physical existence, well-being, a clean environment, preservation of cultural identity, etc. Ole Waever considers national identity to be the most important concept which is not equivalent to state identity, where several peoples can live together within a particular state.[97] Since the end of World War I, national identity has held a dominant position, and it is being strengthened within the EU under the slogan "united in diversity," as "multilingualism and multiculturalism, which are unique to the continent of Europe, are held in high esteem."[98] In the international environment, however, there have always been strong national ideas realized through national liberation struggles and the emergence of nation-states.[99] According to the Copenhagen School, in conditions of globalization and integration, when the borders of society no longer follow the borders of the state, when national legislation and border controls are becoming a thing of the past, it is precisely the consolidation

---

95   Buzan, 1991.
96   Buzan, Wæver, & De Wilde, 1998, p. 119.
97   Dvorakova, K. (2016). Terminology and concepts of immigration policy in Europe and in France. *XLinguae European Scientific Language Journal, 9*(1), 2–23.
98   Bírová, J., & Bubáková, J. (2011). Multikultúra, plurilingvizmus a preklad Charty plurilingvizmu. *XLinguae: Trimestrial European Review, 3*(4), 51–58.
99   Ušiak, J., & Nečas, P. (2011). Societálny a politický sektor v kontexte bezpečnosti štátu. *Politické vedy, 14*(1), 30–49.

of cultural specificity that becomes equivalent to security. This also happens due to the fact that social groups themselves articulate the necessity of protecting their "societal" security. It is important to bear in mind that in the past the emphasis was primarily on the danger to the state; today, the danger to a person as a referent object has been increasingly discussed, and that determines the nature of the potential threats that actors choose as relevant.

Depending on the region and the social standards of the society, these threats may vary considerably, but no one has yet refuted Maslow's model of the hierarchy of human needs (known as *need theory* or *hierarchy theory*), which has existed for more than half a century. The foundation of the imaginary pyramid of needs (declared as universal, which is the weaker and often criticized aspect of the theory) are physiological needs, followed by the need for safety and security, then the need for love, acceptance, belonging, followed by the need for recognition, respect and finally, the need for self-realization. We rank threat characteristics among the most important "facilitating conditions of a security speech act."[100]

In the following research we will focus, besides other things, on the " threatened" needs that Slovak securitizing actors most appeal to in their discourse strategies, and the linguistic means which they consider the most suitable for this purpose. In Western Europe, which is traditionally used to well-being and where the provision of basic physiological needs is taken for granted, it is probably difficult to securitize their threat (in terms of hunger, cold, loss of home, etc.). However, it is possible to productively use the securitization of a "superstructural" need – the threat to the possibility of self-realization. In less prosperous regions, however, the main securitization vector may be directed towards articulating threats to physiological needs, safety, social security, as well as social acceptance, belonging, recognition and respect.

It is precisely these needs (mostly in the poor regions of Slovakia) that are threatened according to the *Republika* movement (analysed in detail in the previous subsection). In recent years, however, we have also observed a new discursive strategy (mostly by right-wing extremists and left-wing populists), which could be described as the securitization of "human dignity" which is allegedly threatened in their target audience (potential voter base) by representatives of the government, politicians, official media, and representatives of liberal, pro-European movements who, according to the aforementioned

---

100   Buzan, Wæver, & De Wilde, 1998, pp. 31–33.

securitizing actors, consistently insult and belittle the so-called "common people."

For the time being, we will give just one example of this type of securitization. In one of her numerous articles published on the disinformation website *Hlavné správy* (Main News), Slavěna Vorobelová, a Slovak MP for the *People's National Socialist Party* (*ĽSNS*), writes: "The Slovak Republic has turned [...] into a fascist dictatorship with a sick vision of the world in which there are citizens of two sorts [...] the bad category are the unvaccinated, dehumanized sub-humans, or misfits, scoundrels, outcasts, cattle, monkeys and trash of society (as some government officials also label them)."[101] The author does not specify which government officials dare to insult citizens in such an expressive manner (if she knew of any specific examples, she would certainly list them; in this case she is just fabricating and misleading) but she makes the readers of *Hlavné správy* feel that their social acceptance, dignity, recognition and respect are threatened, which emerges as a productive discourse strategy (with a powerful persuasive effect).

Securitization intentions are thus identified based on a specific discourse (the preservation of existence, the priority of a certain kind of action, in the sense of "if we don't solve the problem now, then it will be too late, and we won't be able to correct our mistake....) [...] The political presentation of existential threats in this form moves it "above" mainstream politics. In the security discourse, the issue is given a dramatic charge and presented to the public as an issue of the highest priority; being categorized as a security issue, the subject claims the right to deal with the problem using extraordinary measures."[102]

1.5 Securitization as a potential object of research in political linguistics

Political linguistics, which in Slovakia is still at the stage of establishing itself[103] is confronted with the question of how the process of securitization of social phenomena arises in political discourse. It is political linguistics as a theoretically-applied sub-discipline formed at the intersection of political science and

---

101   Vorobelová, S. (2021, November 11). Vakcináckovia idú do finále! *Blog Hlavné správy*. https://blog.hlavnespravy.sk/28477/vakcinackovia-idu-do-finale
102   Cf. Buzan, Wæver, & De Wilde, 1998, p. 24.
103   For more on this topic see Štefančík, Dulebová, 2017 / Cingerová, Dulebová, Štefančík, 2021.

linguistics that could focus not on traditional security issues, but on the analysis of the discursive strategies of the securitizing actors as reflected in speech acts.

"A security argument always involves two predictions: What will happen if we do not take "security action" (the threat), and what will happen if we do (How is the submitted security policy supposed to work?)."[104] The answer to the question of whether the articulated threats are real and whether the proposed security policy has the potential to succeed and deliver the promised result is within the competence of political scientists. The linguist analyses the linguistic means articulating the threat as well as the speech tactics of portraying a "bright future" after the alleged threat is eliminated. The importance of the linguistic component of the research is linked to the fact that a security-oriented speech act does not arise by uttering the word "security." What is essential is the identification of existential threats that require extraordinary measures and the subsequent positive acceptance of this definition by a significant part of the audience (Buzan et al., 1998: 21). Thus, inducing a sense of threat does not have to be "straightforward" and explicit (the words safety, threat, danger do not have to be pronounced), but the metaphors, hyperboles, phrases, expressions with negative connotations, sophisticated historical allusions and impressive linguoculturalisms are able to evoke a sense of threat in the recipient and this is the point where the analysis of discourse strategies and the speech tactics of their use is important. Is the intention to use a given linguistic device related to an attempt to evoke a sense of threat?

The point of departure for the following reflections on the possibilities and directions of politolinguistic research on securitizing discourse is the observation that "for the analyst to grasp this act, the task is not to assess some objective threats that "really" endanger some object to be defended or secured; rather, it is to understand the processes of constructing a shared understanding of what is to be considered and collectively responded to as a threat. The process of securitization is what in language theory is called a speech act. It is not interesting as a sign referring to something more real; it is the utterance itself that is the act. By saying the words, something is done."[105]

Through the use of political science methods and techniques, the vector of analysis is directed at the validity of articulations of "threats" to various entities (the population, democratic values, cultural identity, economic stability, environment, etc.). Within their field of expertise, political scientists

---

104   Buzan, Wæver, & De Wilde, 1998, p. 32.
105   Buzan, Wæver, & De Wilde, 1998, p. 26.

traditionally answer the question of which phenomena become a security issue in the political debate at a given time and why. Equally topical is the question of the social context in which a phenomenon becomes a threat. It can be assumed that some phenomena become threats in the run-up to elections, given that fear is an important factor for mobilizing the electoral vote. Thus, the question for the politological aspect of the research (as part of the politolinguistic method) is whether it is only about this period, or if there are other circumstances that can be defined.

Building on Waever's hypothesis that there is always an elite behind securitization, proponents of social science disciplines have equally focused on the question of who securitizes the selected problems, the attitudes of the main political actors (political parties, especially those in opposition), but also how the phenomenon of civil society, NGOs, etc. is approached. Is there a consensus of opinion among the securitization actors, or is there a traditional coalition-opposition or right-left split? In this context, the question arises whether the actors in this debate include the scientific and academic community and whether the results of research are used as arguments in the debate. For example, in the discussion on climate change, different, even contradictory, studies by different authors are used, while in the discussion on international migration, the results of scientific research are basically marginal in the political discourse. Likewise, the assessment of the success (failure) of securitization as well as the statement of the following process of desecuritization is the competence of political science.

For linguistic analysis, the central question in the topic is "how does it happen?" (by which linguistic means is the speech act carried out that helps to create a sense of threat for the referent objects). Barry Buzan, Ole Wæver and Jaap de Wilde, as political scientists, for obvious reasons avoid "sophisticated linguistic and quantitative techniques".[106] However, political linguistics as a "borderline" discipline using the methods of political science and linguistic analysis in an interdisciplinary approach, has the capacity to go deep into the linguistic aspects of securitization processes and to answer the question of how the process of securitization is linguistically carried out. "The conditions for a successful speech act fall into two categories: (1) internal, linguistic-grammatical – to follow the rules of the act [...] and (2), external, contextual and social – to hold a position from which the act can be made."[107] The former is the province of linguists, the latter of political scientists and discourse analysts.

---

106   Buzan, Wæver, & De Wilde, 1998, p. 176.
107   Buzan, Wæver, & De Wilde, 1998, p. 32.

Strategies of security discourses from the position of the Copenhagen School theory are now being analysed by several researchers both in Slovakia and in the Czech Republic. However, the research is mainly carried out within the framework of political science (or sociology) with the occasional application of methodological procedures of discourse analysis. Although the relevant terminological instruments are used, the research almost never takes on a linguistic dimension, despite the fact that the focus of the analysis is on speech acts and, in this context, on statements made by politicians and other actors of securitization.

For example, in his comprehensive, and from the viewpoint of research methodology, pioneering monograph *Environmental Security in the Czech Republic*,[108] Czech political scientist Petr Martinovský analyzes "the topic of environmental threat perception in the discipline of security studies in the Czech Republic. A modified and updated securitization framework based on the traditional Copenhagen School of Security Studies was used for the analysis and convincingly demonstrates the successful securitization of a number of environmental topics in the Czech Republic[...] the basic conceptual documents of the security policy, public opinion surveys and legislative and institutional emergency measures for the management of environmental threats were used as a source [...] the processes of establishing threats and subsequent securitization were closely monitored."[109] We can see that this is politologically-oriented research, in which even in the process of analysing the establishment of threats and the subsequent securitization, the author does not attempt to delineate the specifics of the speech act in the lexical plane (which is logical given his political science profile). The term speech act itself is only mentioned in a short one-page subsection *7.9.2 Specificity of speech acts in the securitization of agricultural land degradation* (p. 181), but it does not address the particularities of the linguistic means used, but exclusively the dominating content focus of the speech acts.

Another example is Jarmila Androvičová's publication (2015), which analyses the strategies of the security "migration" discourse based on speeches by politicians in the Slovak Parliament and their statements in the media. The author stresses that "in the case of security discourse, it is possible to recognize several commonly used strategies that interact to result in the securitization of migrants. They intertwine, defining migration as a security risk and a cultural

---

108   Martinovský, 2016.
109   Martinovský, p. 14.

threat."[110] She also analyses the basic discursive strategies of securitizing this issue, pointing to negative experiences with migration elsewhere in the world, migrants as a threat to national security and as a global security risk, Slovakia and the countries of Central Europe as a kind of "buffer zone" in relation to Western Europe, negative stereotyping and delegitimization of migrants' intentions and motives, positive self-presentation and denigration of opponents.

In the logical and illustrative delineation and analysis of discourse strategies, Androvičová largely remains on the political science plane, albeit through the example of a number of pithy and relevant statements by specific politicians. She does marginally note that "previous discursive strategies are supported by various rhetorical devices, among which hyperbolization, the use of various similes, and more emotionally-coloured means of expression are very common" (Androvičová, 2015: 82), but she does not indulge in a deeper linguistic analysis. It is here that we see space in similarly nuanced research for the involvement of linguists who are well versed in discourse theory and methodological procedures of discourse analysis as well as the theory of speech acts. They are able to analyse in detail the lexical, stylistic and other peculiarities of a text and draw relevant conclusions on the basis of the analysis of the specific linguistic devices chosen by the given actor. "It is necessary to deal first with the language itself and its inherent manipulative potential, and yet it is often the case that the analysis of texts containing manipulative components is too distant from the linguistic basis."[111] The argumentative practices of threat presentation, for instance, also deserve linguistic analysis. A similar opinion is shared by Czech linguists, suggesting that "the issue of linguistic violence and linguistic manipulation is no longer the exclusive concern of political scientists, sociologists and psychologists, and is experiencing a boom as a relatively new topic in the field of linguistics, which has the methodological tools for the critical analysis of texts and thus enables the understanding and uncovering of the mechanisms of linguistic manipulation and, on their basis, the demystification and demythologization of social and political discourse."[112]

---

110 Androvičová, J. (2017). The migration and refugee crisis in political discourse in Slovakia: Institutionalized securitization and moral panic. *AUC Studia Territorialia*, *16*(2), pp. 39–64.

111 Blaho, M. (2015). Manipulatívny rozmer ruského a slovenského politického diskurzu. In N. Mertová (Ed.), *Hľadanie ekvivalentností VIII*. (pp. 68–73). Prešov: FF PU v Prešove.

112 Gazda, J. (2013). Jazykové prostředky řečové agrese v ruském a českém tisku. In O. Richterek, & M. Půža (Eds.), *Dialog kultur VII. Materiály z mezinárodní vědecké konference* (pp. 84–92). Hradec Králové: Gaudeamus.

Therefore, we see the innovative foundations of Copenhagen School theory as an impetus and theoretical basis for a new scholarly perspective on the notion of security from the position of political linguistics and discourse analysis, allowing us to conceptualize security as a discursive practice that constitutes the political community in whose name it is articulated.

It is essential to bear in mind the textual understanding of securitization as a socially productive speech act that justifies politicians to take urgent measures to neutralize "existential threats" (whether real or merely manifest), while subsequently allowing them to ignore existing rules and procedures. Research with a similar focus would not only be able to explain how a sense of threat is created in referent objects through the speech act, but it would (as a secondary but important impact) help to elucidate the inner workings of the (dis)information war that has been gaining momentum.

II. Employing the tools of corpus linguistics in the analysis of securitization discourse

The use of corpus linguistics tools in securitization research is not yet one of the widespread approaches in this field. This is confirmed by the review study of Stephane J. Baele and Diana Jale,[113] which maps the trend of securitization research on the basis of 171 texts published in 15 major journals in the field of international relations. In it, the authors arrive at the conclusion that the development and enrichment of theory over the past 25 years has occurred at the expense of the development of methodology. *"More than half of the 171 papers (89) were 'primarily theoretical', compared with only 10 'primarily empirical' articles – the remaining being 'balanced theoretically and empirically'"*, they observe.[114] They go on to say that, *"out of the 82 papers with empirical content, only 48 have a clearly identifiable method followed for the analysis,"* with only three papers using a quantitative method.[115] There is thus a clear imbalance between quantitative and qualitative methods, the disadvantages of which have been pointed out in the past.[116]

Examples of studies relying on quantitative methods in recent years include the research of Marek Troszynski and Magdalena El-Ghamari focused on the discourse on migration involving (a) mapping the intensity of reporting on a particular phenomenon in liberal and conservative media, (b) quantitative analysis using tools of corpus linguistics, and (c) qualitative analysis using tools of critical discourse analysis[117]; research on the cognitive construction of security in discourse combining quantitative and qualitative methods[118] and the investigation of Ondřej Heynal and Ľubomír Lupták, which draws on software tools for qualitative analysis.[119]

113 Baele, S. J., & Jalea, D. (2023). Twenty-five years of securitization theory: A corpus-based review. *Political Studies Review, 21*(2), 376–389.

114 Baele, & Jalea, 2023.

115 Baele, & Jalea, 2023.

116 Baele, S. J., & Thomson, C. P. (2017). An experimental agenda for securitization theory. *International Studies Review, 19*(4), 646–666.

117 Troszyński, M., & El-Ghamari, M. (2022). A great divide: Polish media discourse on migration, 2015-2018. *Humanities and Social Sciences Communications*, 9, 1–12.

118 Hu Ch. (2023). A corpus-based study on the cognitive construction of security in discourse. *Frontiers in Psychology*, 13, 1–13.

119 Hejnal, O., & Lupták, Ľ. (2013). Využitie CAQDAS pri výskume sekuritizácie. In J. Ušiak, J. Lasicová, & D. Kollár (Eds.), *Bezpečnostné fórum 2013 – Security forum 2013* (pp. 232–239). Banská Bystrica: Fakulta politických vied a medzinárodních vzťahov Univerzita Mateja Bela v Banskej Bystrici.

We regard as particularly inspiring the procedure presented in the research of Troszynski and El-Ghamari, whose approach recognizes different possibilities of quantitative and qualitative analysis and their relatedness.

In our reflections on the possibilities of using corpus analysis tools, we proceed from the fact that the attention of scholars concerned with the issue of securitization in broader scope research is focused not only on individual utterances or texts, but also on "virtual units extending beyond the level of the text, whose composition is determined by widely understood content (semantic) criteria"[120] – on discourses. And these entities – following their definition, have many points of contact with another transtextual entity – corpus, i.e., "an electronic, systematically constructed and organized collection of texts".[121]. The distinction between discourse analysis, which involves not only the method but also the theoretical conceptualization of discourse issues, and corpus linguistics provides, in our view, a solid understanding of the questions that can be answered by working with a corpus and how to structure the research process.[122]

Corpus linguistics:

- works with fragments of text, the statements are samples of discourses;
- research is primarily quantitative, qualitative analysis is considered only as a complement to quantitatively oriented research;
- focuses on form and grammar;
- division of work in accordance with the stages of research (text generation, text processing, text analysis); and
- access to data is generally not restricted, it is public.[123]

Discourse analysis:

- operates with the notion of a single text, the utterances are textually and discursively bound;

---

120   Busse, D., & Teubert, W. (2013). Ist Diskurs ein sprachwissenschaftliches Objekt? Zur Methodenfrage der historischen Semantik. In D. Busse, & W. Teubert (Eds.), *Linguistische Diskursnanalyse: neue Perspektiven* (pp. 13–30). Wiesbaden: Springer VS.

121   Čermák, F. (2017). *Korpus a korpusová lingvistika*. Praha: Karolinum, p. 10.

122   The text below contains a comparison conducted by J. Spitzmüller and I. H. Warnke, relying on G.N. Leech. cf. Spitzmüller, J., & Warnke, I. H. (2011). *Diskurslinguistik. Eine Einführung in Theorien und Methoden der transtextuellen Sprachanalyse*. Berlin, Boston: Walter de Gruyter, and Leech, G. N. (2000). Grammar of Spoken English. New Outcomes of Corpus-oriented Research. *Language Learning, 50*(4), 675–724

123   Spitzmüller, J., & Warnke, p. 32 / Leech, 2000.

- research is primarily qualitative, quantitative analysis is regarded only as a complement to qualitatively oriented research;
- focuses on content and semantics;
- there is no division of work in accordance with the stages of research (text generation, text processing, text analysis); and
- as a rule, access to data is restricted, non-public.[124]

In terms of our research, the quantitative-qualitative, fragment-text, form-content distinctions were important to us. Thus, the tools and procedures of corpus linguistics can serve as a starting point for qualitative research or complement it in the final stage.

Possible approaches to the analysis of texts, as fragments of discourse/corpus, were seen in two directions.

In the first case, it is a procedure in which attention is focused on the profile of key lexical units belonging to the semantic field "security." Pursuant to an extended definition, semantic fields are seen following "a set of related concepts, typically lexicalized concepts in paradigmatic relation to one another"[125] and in the Sketchengine manager they can be generated via the Thesaurus function, which allows the construction of a list of words based on the context in which they appear in the selected text corpus[126]. Our research features the use of three parallel corpora. The ELEXIS Slovak Web 2021 is general and has 1,198,933,594 tokens. The second corpus consisted of texts published in the online version of the Denník N. newspaper from 2015 to 2022 (DN Corpus), which was coded by us as a liberal periodical. It has 4,945,313 tokens. The third corpus has a comparable size of 4,848,197 tokens and is compiled from texts (including blogs) published in the online periodical Hlavné správy from 2013 to 2022 (HS Corpus), which was coded as an anti-liberal periodical (and a popular conspiracy and disinformation website).[127] We were interested whether the semantic fields generated based on different corpora would differ. The results are presented below.

Thesaurus entry for "hrozba" [**threat**] (first 10 positions)

Table 1: General corpus (ELEXIS Slovak Web 2021), visualisation by SketchEngine, translated by authors

---

124   Spitzmüller, J., & Warnke, p. 32 / Leech, 2000.

125   Murphy, L. M., & Koskela, A. (2010). *Key terms in semantics*. London, New York: Continuum International Publishing Group.

126   Sketchengine. https://www.sketchengine.eu/guide/thesaurus-synonyms-antonyms-similar-words

127   cf. the list of sites with controversial content on a monitoring portal konspiratori.sk. Available on Konspiratori. https://konspiratori.sk/zoznam-stranok.

Table 1

threat (*hrozba*)	0	
danger (*nebezpečenstvo*)	0.380	44,986
risk (*riziko*)	0.300	195,403
consequence (*následok*)	0.282	84,835
menace (*ohrozenie*)	0.279	31,585
outcome (*dôsledok*)	0.261	204,648
disaster (*katastrofa*)	0.238	27,403
significance (*význam*)	0.236	145,107
violence (*násilie*)	0.236	43,767
benefits (*prínos*)	0.230	50,782
influence (*vplyv*)	0.230	249,166

Table 2: DN Corpus (visualisation by SketchEngine, translated by authors)

Table 2 Threat 232x

threat (*hrozba*)	0	
consequence (*následok*)	0.145	253
risk (*riziko*)	0.140	488
benefits (*prínos*)	0.137	152
challenge (*výzva*)	0.135	544
danger (*nebezpečenstvo*)	0.121	134
epidemic (*epidémia*)	0.120	179
competition (*konkurencia*)	0.119	289
advertisement (*reklama*)	0.119	367
to threaten (*hroziť*)	0.118	350

Table 2   Fortsetzung

doubt (*pochybnosť*)	0.117	181

Table 3: HS Corpus (visualisation by SketchEngine, translated by authors)

Table 3   Threat 835x

threat (*hrozba*)	0	
danger (*nebezpečenstvo*)	0.266	304
problem (*problém*)	0.252	3,176
enemy (*nepriateľ*)	0.245	573
influence (*vplyv*)	0.241	951
force (*sila*)	0.223	2,480
war (*vojna*)	0.223	2,925
conflict (*konflikt*)	0.223	1,092
challenge (*výzva*)	0.222	875
activity (*aktivita*)	0.221	888
task (*úloha*)	0.219	1,562

The comparison indicates that the HS Corpus can be considered to have an almost fourfold higher frequency of use of the unit. One can also gain some insight into the conceptualization of "threat" by comparing the list of words based on the context in which they appear. In the case of the HS Corpus, units belonging to the conflictogenic discourse appear in higher positions than the units with the highest degree of similarity; "threat" is conceptualized in a more exacerbated way, and placed in similar contexts as "danger" (in the DN Corpus in 5th place, similarity: 0.12), "problem" (in the DN Corpus in 230th place, similarity: 0.07), "enemy" (in the DN Corpus in 17th place, similarity: 0.11), "influence" (in the DN Corpus in 180th place, similarity: 0.08), "force" (in the DN Corpus in 375th place, similarity: 0.07), "war" (in the DN Corpus in 281st place, similarity: 0.07), "conflict" (in the DN Corpus in 161st place, similarity: 0.08). Importantly, in the case of the DN Corpus, we see a more frequent use of the unit "challenge," a frequent euphemism applied in place of the unit "problem". An interesting finding for us was that in the case of the DN Corpus, "threat" is used in the same contexts as "epidemic" (the Corpus captures the discourse of the Covid-19 pandemic period), while in the HS Corpus the unit "pandemic" appears in as many as 122 positions (similarity: 0.17, "epidemic" does not appear in any of the more than 1,000 positions of the list). In our view, the high positioning of the unit "influence" is also relevant. It has a different profile in the corpora studied[128] – in the HS corpus, its negative connotation and its placement in narratives about spheres (of influence) significantly come to the fore.

Profile of the unit "vplyv" (influence)

Table 4: HS Corpus (visualisation by SketchEngine)

Table 4

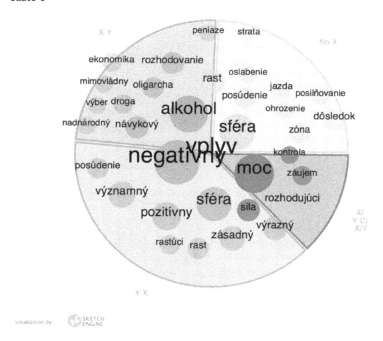

DN Corpus (visualisation by SketchEngine)

---

128   The profile of selected units was abstracted using the Wordsketch function which enabled us to fix collocations of a chosen word and other words in its surrounding, its "collocational behavior". Cf Sketchengine. https://www.sketchengine.eu/guide/word-sketch-collocations-and-word-combinations

Table 5

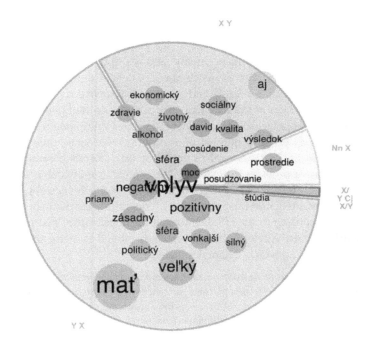

visualization by

An intriguing finding was that for both sub-corpora, the lemma "safety" occurred mainly in the same contexts as negatively connoted words, which is at variance with the results from the general corpus.

However, from our perspective, the tools of corpus linguistics proved most beneficial in verifying frequent metaphorical expressions fixed in previous research into the securitization language of groups coded as right-wing extremists and left-wing populists.

Securitization discourse primarily uses metaphors of a conflictogenic nature as manifestations of explicit speech aggression and the most effective tool of "securitization tactics". First of all, these metaphorical concepts are morbial, zoomorphic, of natural elements, anthropomorphic, beastly, sexual, sporting, criminal, military, theatrical. When selecting specific models for the purpose of corpus analysis, the already described/analysed, and partially systematized and hierarchized metaphorical concepts of hate speech from the investigations of A. Chudinov,[129] Baranov, Karaulov,[130] Molnárová, Lauková,[131] Vershinina,[132] Baranova,[133] Cingerová, Dulebová,[134] Riaposova,[135] Voroshilova,[136] etc. can be helpful

The beastly metaphor of *Satan* as an explicit even "naive" (primal) way of demonizing the opponent/enemy and its intentions, especially in the public discourse of a state in which almost 70 % of the population is Roman Catholic[137] represents a reliable and short path to evoke repulsive associations in the consciousness of the recipient. The analysis of the HS corpus shows the extraordinary popularity of this model (105 times, compared to which the DN corpus shows a negligible number of uses of the term Satan, only 14 times, 2 of which were in the metaphorical pejorative sense). Corpus-based exploration is useful because it provides the clarity of the context, from which it can be clearly seen what is presented as a "threat" to the securitized reference object. The most popular phrase in demonizing the "other"/"enemy" turned out to be "the services of Satan"; according to the HS disinformation website, the "main servants" are the world Zionist-Anglo-Saxon power elites, liberal fascism, the mainstream media, the EU and NGOs. Examples include:

> SL → *liberálny fašizmus a hlavne mainstreamové média okrem toho, že sú* **službníkmi**
> **Satana***, sú skutočnými konšpirátormi a zároveň šíriteľmi liberálno-fašistickej ideológie/*
> *Globálny* **parazit***, t.j. svetovládne sionisticko-anglosaské mocenské elity* **v službách**
> **Satana***, ako aj ich slovenskí* **prisluhovači na čele s primadonou** *sa opäť rozbesneli/*

129 Chudinov, A. P. (2013). *Ocherki po sovremennoy politicheskoy metaforologii.* Yekaterinburg: Ural State Pedagogical University.
130 Baranov, A. N., & Karaulov, J. N. (1994). *Slovar russkikh politicheskikh metafor.* Moskva: Pomovskii i partnery.
131 Molnárová, E., & Lauková, J. (2018). *Jazykový obraz migrácie v nemeckom masmediálnom diskurze.* Banská Bystrica: Belianum.
132 Vershinina, T. (2002). *Zoomorfnaya, fitomorfnaya i antropomorfnaya metafora v sovremennom politicheskom diskurse.* Yekaterinburg: Ural State Pedagogical University.
133 Baranov, A. (2011). *Korruptsiya: netraditsionniy vzglyad. Metaforicheskiye grani korruptsii.* Moskva: Institut Russkogo Jazyka Vinogradova.
134 Cingerová, & Dulebová, 2019.
135 Riaposova, A. (2002). *Metaforicheskiye modeli s agressivnym pragmaticheskim potentsialom.* Jekaterinburg: Uralsky Federalnyj Universitet.
136 Voroshilova, M. (2016). *Kreolizirovannaya metafora kak orudiye diskreditatsii.* Yekaterinburg: Ural State Pedagogical University.
137 Štatistické sčítanie obyvateľov, domov a bytov (2021). Náboženské vyznanie. https://www.scitanie.sk/k-rimskokatolickemu-vyznaniu-sa-prihlasilo-56-obyvatelov

Cyril a Metod bez svätožiary a krížov? Európsku úniu **ovláda satan** *alebo* **satanizmus** */Služobníci Satana opäť na nás vycerili svoj zubiská. Nech si ich dolámu! / Takmer všetky tromfy (hlavne peniaze a mediálny priestor) majú v rukách liberálni fašisti. Čo urobia predstavitelia kresťanských cirkví na Slovensku, aby eliminovali ich silu a odhalili pravú* **tvár Satana?** */* **Veľký Satan** *prostredníctvom svojho najväčšieho a najsilnejšieho otroka USA viedol vojny, vytváral chaos, dosadzoval svojich poskokov do čela štátov, firiem a korporácii, vysával životodárnu miazgu národov. Stále silnejší,* **financoval svojich mimovládnych sataníkov** *všade po svete.../ Klin do tlačiarničky na doláriky, to je* **klin do srdca Veľkého Satana** *a klin do srdca to je smrť/ nastolenie celosvetového globálneho fašizmu NWO (Nový svetový poriadok), ktorého dôsledkom by mal byť doteraz v histórii nevídaný krutý teror a vraždenie v stámiliónoch – hlavne my kresťania sme znovu hlavným terčom týchto zámerov, lebo stojíme na strane Ježiša Krista, ktorý je zasa* **hlavným terčom nenávisti Satana** *a ktorý sa nás chystá zničiť cez dva svoje najmocnejšie politické nástroje – svetovládny sionizmus a islam. USA a jeho moc sa mali stať nástrojom v rukách sionistov, kde malo dôjsť k nastoleniu krutého fašistického teroru a vraždenia odporcov/ v Západnej Európe už nás kresťanov a Ježiša Krista nenávidia všetci, lebo ich nenávisť je* **odrazom nenávisti Satana** *, ktorému slúžia, a tak začali likvidovať kresťanské symboly, búrať kresťanské kostoly, prípadne ich prestavovať na mešity, ktoré podobne ako "no-go" zóny rastú ako huby po daždi.*[138]

---

138 EL → in addition to being **the servants of Satan**, liberal fascism and especially the mainstream media are real conspirators and propagators of liberal-fascist ideology/ The global **parasite**, i.e., the world-governing Zionist-Anglo-Saxon power elites **in the service of Satan**, as well as their Slovak **minions, headed by the prima donna**, have gone wild once again/ Cyril and Methodius without haloes and crosses? The European Union is **controlled by Satan** or **Satanism /Satan's servants** have once again bared their teeth at us. Let them break their teeth! / Almost all the aces (especially money and media space) are in the hands of liberal fascists. What will the leaders of the Christian churches in Slovakia do to eliminate their power and expose the true **face of Satan**?/ **The Great Satan**, through his greatest and most powerful slave, the USA, has waged wars, created chaos, put his minions in charge of countries, companies and corporations, sucking the life-giving sap of nations. Ever more powerful, he **has funded his non-governmental Satan offspring** all over the world.../ A wedge in the dollar printing press is **a wedge in the heart of the Great Satan** and a wedge in the heart – that is death / establishing the worldwide global fascism of the NWO (New World Order), which should result in cruel terror and murder in the hundreds of millions unprecedented in history – we, Christians, in particular, are once again the main target of these intentions, because we are on the side of Jesus Christ, who in turn is **the main target of Satan's hatred** and who is about to destroy us through two of his most powerful political instruments – world-governing Zionism and Islam. The USA and its power was to become a tool in the hands of Zionists, where cruel fascist terror and the murder of opponents was to

The use of zoomorphic metaphors as a method of dehumanizing the enemy and its actions has a long tradition, to which a number of studies in the field of metaphorology have been dedicated.[139] They include the research of Kateryny Korotych[140] "on the material of Ukrainian Soviet, pro-German and nationalistic press of World War II, the author characterizes features of manifestation and pragmatic loading of the zoomorphic metaphors which designate the enemy. The author found that zoomorphic metaphors appeared to be a universal means of creation of an image of the enemy in the Soviet, pro-German and nationalistic discourses; their language representations are similar and have only some differences" (Korotych, 2016: 352). In the process of excerpting and analysing the use of zoomorphic metaphors from 1941 to1945, the author came to the conclusion that metaphors with negative connotations (*wolves, jackals, monkeys, pigs, dogs, hyenas, vultures, crows, snakes, sharks*, etc.) proved to be the most productive. Anatoliy Chudinov, one of the founders of Russian political linguistics, and the author of his fundamental work "Russia in the Mirror of Metaphor"[141] reaches the conclusion that zoomorphic metaphors are the most traditional and widespread in Russian political discourse and few of them have positive semantics.[142] Galina Sklyarevskaya[143] also concludes that zoomorphic metaphors aim at "discrediting, marginalizing the object [of speech] and possess pejorative coloring".

---

be imposed/ In Western Europe, Christians and Jesus Christ are already hated by all, because their hatred is **a reflection of the hatred of Satan**, to whom they serve, and so they began to destroy Christian symbols, demolish Christian churches, or convert them into mosques, which, like "no-go" zones, are growing like mushrooms after the rain.

139   Besides the aforementioned studies, the specifics of zoomorphic metaphor are analysed in the works of, e.g., Krupa, V. (1990). *Metafora na rozhraní vedeckých disciplín.* Bratislava: Tatran / Sakalauskaite A. (2010). *Zoometaphors in English, German, and Lithuanian: A Corpus Study.* Berkeley: University of California / Sommer R., & Sommer B. (2011). Zoomorphy: Animal Metaphors for Human Personality. *Antropozoos, 24*(3), 237–248.

140   Korotych, V. (2016). Zoomorphic Metaphor as a Mean of Creation of an Image of the Enemy in the Ukrainian Press of 1941–1945. *Studia-linguistica, 9.*

141   Chudinov, A. (2001). *Rossiya v metaforicheskom zerkale: Kognitivnoye issledovaniye politicheskoy metafori.* Yekaterinburg. Ural State Pedagogical University.

142   Chudinov, 2001, p. 136.

143   Sklyarevskaya, G. N. (1993). *Metaphor in the System of Language.* Sankt Peterburg: Nauka, p. 91.

This tendency is also confirmed by our corpus research into HS and DN, with quantitative indicators leading us to the conclusion that the HS disinformation website uses zoomorphic metaphors (with the intention to primarily discredit the opponent at the level of emotion) significantly more often than DN. We will demonstrate this through the most frequent metaphors (it is essential to bear in mind that the use of animal names is not always metaphorical and thus relevant to our research).

In the analysed HS corpus, the word *monkey* occurs 51 times (47 times in the metaphorical pejorative sense), in the DN corpus (which maps the same period and contains approximately the same number of tokens) it occurs only 26 times (16 times in the metaphorical sense); thus, we can see that the ratio of the conflicting metaphor monkey is 3:1 "in favour" of the HS corpus. Moreover, an unexpected finding is that the authors of HS quite often purposely "put" the monkey metaphor in the mouths of their opponents, who supposedly perceive/name people from socially weaker classes and less educated people in this way (and therefore a priori insult the majority of HS readers):

SL → *Druhou, tou zlou, kategóriou sú neočkovaní dehumanizovaní podľudia, resp. dezoláti, grázli, vyvrheli, **dobytok, opice** a odpad spoločnosti (ako ich označujú aj niektorí vládni činitelia), ktorí už do "vakcináckovskej" spoločnosti proste nepatria / odkiaľ sa vzala toľká nenávisť, odkiaľ ju má, ako je možné, že delí spoločnosť na nadľudí a **opice** / zo spoločnosti bohatých a úspešných a ostatní sú chudáci a **opice**/ Čaputová vyhrala a prvé čo spraví je, že zatočí s **opicami** a antisemitami, ako ste vy / veľmi progresívny, ktorý rozdeľuje spoločnosť na bohatých, úspešných a neúspešné zaostalé opice, ktoré by ani nemali existovať, lebo zavadzajú.* The unflattering image of the monkey is also used with the classic aim of defaming opponents: *Preto aj tie post hodnotenia po voľbách, ktoré pokračujú v lineárnom marše vymývania mozgov, klamania, škatuľkovania, **démonizovania hodnotiacich opíc a papagájov** systému / Cvičená **americká opica** Kiska, je najvyšším predstaviteľom vojnového štváčstva. Na základe vymyslenej a neopodstatnenej ruskej hrozby, pod vymyslenou ochranou demokracie, ktorá je v skutočnosti americko – sionistickou vojenskou agresiou s cieľom zničiť Slovanov, zničiť Rusko, zničiť slovanské európske štáty, vrátane Slovenska / Gejurópa sa úplne vyšinula so svojimi gejpochodmi a homosexuálnymi sobášmi. Vy ani nechápete, že sa meníte na **opice**.*[144]

---

144   EL → The second, the bad, category are the unvaccinated dehumanized subhumans, that is "the trash", scoundrels, outcasts, **cattle, monkeys** and waste of society (as some government officials call them), who simply do not belong in the "vaccinazi" society anymore / where does so much hatred come from, where does the society get it, how come it divides the society into superhumans and **monkeys** / from the society of the rich and successful and the rest are losers and **monkeys** / Čaputová won and the first thing she will do is to curb the **monkeys** and antisemites like you / a very progressive one that divides society into rich, successful and unsuccessful backward **monkeys**

There are also instances of the use of metaphors in the form of phrasemes (*the gentleman wanted to show at all costs in Brussels how far behind the monkeys* [literal translation of a Slovak phraseme which means: to be underdeveloped, authors' note] *we are in Czechoslovakia*). The corpus also contains intertextual references, for example in the form of film allusions (*After the cortex has died completely when you start to believe that you are on Olympus and not on **the planet of the apes**, your time has come. You will become a loyal picker of designed news – that is, an elite journalist. The others are conspirators*).

Traditionally stigmatizing is the hyena metaphor, which occurs up to 24 times in the HS corpus (24 times in the negative metaphorical sense); in the DN corpus it is found only 10 times (8 times in the metaphorical sense), which again demonstrates the threefold prevalence of the "hate speech" metaphor in the HS corpus. Hyenas in the HS corpus are mostly defined as *European, media, global, political, presidential*. The characteristics of hyenas according to HS are: *corrupt traitors, warmongers, Judases, Soros people, sun-worshippers, truth-lovers, humanitarian bombers, human-rights demagogues, **media hyenas***. Meanwhile, imagery abounds among the authors of HS news texts:

> SL → *zorganizovaná atmosféra paniky a strachu, na ktorej majú, okrem **globálnych hyen**, podiel politici národných štátov / Aby sa úplne dorazil tento malý chudobný Slovensky štát, **hyeny z Európskej únie** a ich spojenci tiež potrebujú zneužiť a zotročiť Slovákov / otázka okolo nákupu testov – komu vlastne priniesli osoh? ľudom, či **nenažratým hyenám**, bažiacim iba po zisku / Celá Európa plače až kvíli, trhaná na kusy, ako je obeť **trhaná hyenami**, a to ešte za živa. Rozhodnutia privilegovanej menšiny sa snažia zadupať našu identitu / zevolucionalizovaná **prezidentská hyena** / **Európska hyena** nemení svoju kožu ani povahu. Iba patrónov.*[145]

---

that shouldn't even exist because they stand in the way. The unflattering image of the monkey is also used with the classic aim of defaming opponents: Hence even those post-election evaluations that continue the linear march of brainwashing, lying, pigeonholing, **demonizing of the rating monkeys and parrots** of the system / The trained **American monkey, Kiska**, is the ultimate representative of warmongering. Based on a fabricated and unfounded Russian threat, under the fabricated protection of democracy, which in reality is American-Zionist military aggression to destroy the Slavs, to destroy Russia, to destroy the Slavic European states, including Slovakia / Gayrope has gone completely insane with its gay parades and homosexual marriages. You don't even understand that you are turning into **monkeys**.

145   EL → the organized atmosphere of panic and fear, in which, in addition to **the global hyenas**, the politicians of the nation states have a share / In order to completely finish off this poor little Slovak state, **the hyenas from the European Union** and their allies also need to exploit and enslave Slovaks / the question regarding the test

One of the popular metaphors with negative connotations is the *shark* metaphor; it occurs 24 times in the HS corpus, 14 times in the figurative sense (mostly with the adjectives: financial, investment, world). In DN, the lexeme *shark* appears only 16 times, just once in the metaphorical sense. The repulsive image of a vulture projected onto an enemy is found 7 times in HS (out of 9 occurrences), in DN the lexeme *vulture* occurs only 5 times, and only once in the metaphorical sense.

The lexeme *octopus* is encountered 16 times in the DN corpus, 7 of which are metaphorical, while in the HS it is found 34 times and it is used in a figurative (negative) sense as many as 29 times (*the octopus of NGOs, mafia, oligarchic, corrupt, American, Soros,* etc.). Hence, the corpus research clearly illustrates the significant prevalence of zoomorphic metaphors with negative semantics in the HS disinformation corpus.

In terms of our research (the process of securitization in language), metaphors with a markedly negative connotation logically appear in the centre of attention, yet we keep in mind the fact that metaphors can be twofold – alive and dead, i.e., lexicalized. "The alive may vary according to their degree of conventionality, but as carriers of language we identify them as figurative expressions. Lexicalized or dead metaphors are not identified as metaphors (with figurative meanings) by language carriers, but are used as ready-made language patterns of a given linguaculture."[146] Their insubstantial, persuasive effect seemingly puts them in a marginal position in the process of researching the language of securitization, but in the negative context of intimidation, even dead metaphors tend to gain in expressiveness. For example, the lexicalized metaphor of *wave* is encountered 458 times in the HS corpus, including *migration wave* (44), *refugee wave* (11), *immigration wave* (6), *wave of resistance* (14), *wave of disaffection* (4), *wave of anger* (4). For instance:

SL → *ide o "genocídu" obyvateľstva EÚ* **migračnými vlnami** / *Bezpečnostnú hrozbu predstavuje aj možná infiltrácia* **migračnej a utečeneckej vlny** *osobami sympatizujúcimi s radikálnymi a teroristickými organizáciami/ nebývalá* **vlna odporu** *proti bezbrehej a neriadenej migrácii a scestnému multikulturalizmu, prinášajúcemu množstvo bezpečnostných rizík / Keď sa dvíha*

---

purchases – who did they actually benefit? people, or **gluttonous hyenas**, seeking only profit / All of Europe is weeping and wailing, tearing to pieces, like **hyenas tear their victim** apart while it is still alive. The decisions of the privileged minority try to trample on our identity / the revolutionized **presidential hyena** / **the European hyena** does not change its skin or its nature. Only the patrons.

146   Cingerová, Dulebová, & Štefančík, 2021.

vlna národného hnevu, zmätie všetko. Pred našimi očami sa udialo rozbitie ZSSR, Juhoslávie, NDR, Varšavskej zmluvy. To isté sa môže stať aj s NATO či EU.[147]

It occurs 510 times in the DN corpus, but predominantly as a physics term, and as a societal domain metaphor considerably less than in HS (refugee 5x, migration 9x).

The explicitly conflictogenic metaphors include criminal imagery, with the terms *mafia* and *crime* being the most frequent, as our previous research revealed. The corpus research shows a significant predominance of these lexemes in HS (mafia 345x, crime 718x) compared to DN (mafia 74x, crime 221x).

In connection with "crime" in HS, the most frequent phrases are: war crime (95x), organized (76x), migrant (4x), monstrous (4x), Ukrainian (5x). The most frequent connections in DN are: organized (25x), war (10x), environmental (4x), crimes against humanity (6x), crimes of communism (10x). Examples of the most typical contextualization in HS are the following:

SL → *môžeme hovoriť o* **zločinoch** *kapitalizmu,* **zločinoch** *demokracie a* **zločinoch** *liberalizmu, pretože obludné* **zločiny** *s miliónmi obetí sa diali a dejú aj v režimoch hlásiacich sa ku kapitalizmu, demokracii a liberalizmu / množstvo dôkazov o zámernom páchaní* **ukrajinských zločinov** *proti civilom/ ide o ďalší dôkaz podpory páchania* **ukrajinských zločinov** **NATO**. *Nie je to žiadne prekvapenie, keďže* **NATO je zločinecká organizácia** *hájaca záujmy USA a ktorá slúži na* **legalizáciu zločinov USA** *touto medzinárodnou organizáciou.*[148]

As for the *mafia* metaphor, in HS the most common phrases are *liberal-fascist mafia* (14x), *criminal mafia* (12x), *gorilla mafia* (11x), *judicial mafia* (5x), *media mafia* (4x), *transnational mafia* (3x), *liberal mafia* (4x). The only recurrent

---

147 EL → it is the "genocide" of the EU population by **migratory waves** / The possible infiltration of **the migratory and refugee waves** by persons sympathizing with radical and terrorist organizations also poses a security threat/ an unprecedented **wave of resistance** against unrestricted and uncontrolled migration and misguided multiculturalism, which brings numerous security risks / When **a wave of national anger** rises, it will sweep everything away. Before our eyes, the disintegration of the USSR, Yugoslavia, the GDR, the Warsaw Pact took place. The same can happen to NATO or the EU.

148 EL → we can talk about **crimes** of capitalism, **crimes** of democracy and **crimes** of liberalism, because monstrous **crimes** with millions of victims have happened and are happening in regimes adhering to capitalism, democracy and liberalism / abundant evidence of deliberate **Ukrainian crimes** against civilians / This is further evidence of **NATO's support for** the perpetration of **Ukraine's crimes**. This is no surprise, as **NATO is a criminal organization** defending US interests and serves to legalize the crimes of the US by this international organization.

phrases in DN were *Italian mafia* (10x) and *the bankruptcy mafia* (4x). In our opinion, the main directions of contextualization of the mafia metaphor in the HS corpus are most succinctly reflected by the following examples:

SL → **Liberálno-fašistická mafia** *demonštruje svoju moc a silný politický tlak aj v súvislosti s vykonštruovaným procesom vyšetrovania obvinených Mariána Kočnera a spol./ do vyšetrovacích orgánov a prokuratúry* **liberálno-fašistická mafia** *nielen prenikla, ale ich má aj pod svojou kontrolou. Pod patronátom zahraničných tajných služieb pracujúcich pre elity globálneho fašizmu / Biela rasa je ohrozená najmä rasistami, medzinárodným terorizmom,* **zločineckou mafiou**, *ekonomickou genocídou, mediálnou manipuláciou, legalizáciou nezákonnej a násilnej migrácie/ zločinci – politici, s nimi prepojení zločinci,* **justičná mafia** *atď. / Ukrajina je dnes zločinecký štát, totálna korupcia, totálny zločin. Ich* **organizované mafie**, *ktoré rozkrádajú pomoc z EÚ a USA, sa dnes vyvážajú za svojimi biznismi na drahých autách po celej Európe / je namočený v službách pre skorumpovaných politikov, politickú a* **mediálnu mafiu**, *nájomných novinárov a nájomné vraždy. Denník SME spáchal* **mafiánsku objednávku**, *úmyselnú manipuláciu, cenzúru a mediálny podvod / dosadené skorumpované vlády národných štátov sa prizerajú ako kántria obyvateľstvo, ekonomiku a preformátovávajú život podľa toho ako to* **nadnárodné mafie** *naplánovali. To všetko za gigantickej masáže masmédií opäť vlastnenými tými istými* **zahraničnými nadnárodnými mafiami** */ Vyšetrovatelia a prokurátori, ktorí nie sú agentmi* **liberálnej mafie** *pri tzv. "vyšetrovaní" vraždy, sú pod šialeným tlakom* **mediálnych špinavcov** *tak zastrašení, že radšej spolupracujú pri vznášaní účelových obvinení len nech majú od* **mediálneho diabla** *svätý pokoj.*[149]

---

149   EL → **The liberal-fascist mafia** demonstrates its power and strong political pressure also in respect of the fabricated process of the investigation of the accused Marián Kočner and Co. / **the liberal-fascist mafia** has not only infiltrated the investigative bodies and the prosecutor's office, but it even controls them. Under the patronage of foreign intelligence services working for the elites of global fascism / The white race is threatened mainly by racists, international terrorism, **criminal mafia**, economic genocide, media manipulation, the legalization of unlawful and forced migration / criminals – politicians, criminals connected to them, **judicial mafia**, etc. / Ukraine today is a criminal state, total corruption, total crime. Their organized mafias, which steal aid coming from the EU and the US, are now using expensive cars to pursue their business all over Europe / is soaked in services for corrupt politicians, the political and **media mafia**, hired journalists and assassinations. The SME newspaper perpetrated a **mafia order**, deliberate manipulation, censorship and media fraud / the installed corrupt governments of nation-states are watching as they decimate the population, the economy, and reshape life the way **the transnational mafias** planned. All this backed by a gigantic campaign of the mass media – owned by the same **foreign transnational mafias** / Investigators and prosecutors who are not agents of the **liberal mafia** in the so-called "investigation" of the murder are so intimidated by the insane pressure of the **media scum** that they prefer to cooperate in bringing purposely-built charges just to be left alone by the **media devil**.

The analysis of frequent metaphorical patterns already identified in previous research on the securitization language of right-wing extremists and left-wing populists using the Sketchengine corpus manager has convincingly demonstrated the distinct prevalence of metaphors with negative semantics in the corpus of the HS disinformation website, as well as their frequency and the relatively stable collocations in which they function and are incorporated into the specific language of hate speech. In this respect, the tools of corpus linguistics can be regarded as a suitable complement to qualitative research.

III. Speech acts of Ľuboš Blaha as a prototype of the securitisation strategies of leftist populism

Fear consolidates, artificially induced fear can become the basis for a successful political strategy, and at the same time it is easy "to understand people's fears, because fear is a deeply human emotion. What is not a deeply human emotion, however, is the desire to deliberately misuse anger and fear, or to exploit the issue to unleash hatred against other people, or to saddle that wave of hatred. Such people do not want to unite, they do not need to gain trust, they are content with simply undermining trust in everything. In the civil service, in institutions, in science, in medicine" (from the speech of President Zuzana Čaputová on the state of the republic in the plenary session of the National Assembly of the Slovak Republic, September 28, 2021).

The research in this first part of the chapter focuses on the analysis of speech acts in the social networks of Ľuboš Blaha, the successful representative of Slovak left-wing populism, the deputy chairman of the opposition (in 2020–2023) SMER party, in the process of the securitization of vaccination in 2021, by means of examples of speeches concentrating on the metaphorical modelling of this sharply discussed social issue. Subsequently, in order to compare securitization vectors and analyse the dynamics of speech strategies (for the same securitization actor), examples of Blaha's speech acts from 2023 (when the number of "endangered entities" in the discourse of the left populists is increasing at a remarkable pace in view of the pre-term parliamentary elections on September 30, 2023) are also discussed.

This analysis is not of a political science nature (it does not evaluate political intentions or the social relevance of the statements' content), nor does it examine in which cases the statements are conspiracy theories, hoaxes, deliberate trolling, fabulation, purposeful lying, etc. Its focus is solely on the linguistic (lexical) level of the speeches, through which we seek to show how the securitisation of vaccination was realized in the specific texts of a well-known leftist populist (an influential actor of securitisation who had 156,000 followers on Facebook in 2021), with regard to the intentions of the use of specific metaphorical models.

This analysis has an interdisciplinary, namely politolinguistic, orientation with an overlap into media linguistics (online media as an object of research), discourse analysis (implicit and explicit discourse strategies of using specific linguistic means), cognitive linguistics (metaphor as a way of cognition, conceptualization and evaluation of the world) and linguoculturology (focus on the specificities of the Slovak linguistic image of the world and the perception of some metaphors as linguoculturemes).

Methodologically, we rely on the innovative premises of the Copenhagen School's theory of securitization, allowing us to conceptualize security as a discursive practice and perceiving the act of securitization as a speech act that generates new meanings and is able to set in motion certain social dynamics. What is important is the conception of securitization as a socially productive speech act that legitimizes the right of politicians to take urgent action to neutralize "existential threats" (whether real or merely manifested), while allowing them to ignore existing rules and procedures:

> SL → *Ostáva len ulica, nepokoje, blokády, štrajky / Ten výbuch bude počuť v celej Európe / my ako slovenskí ľavičiari povedieme národ do boja / Smer bude počas jesene zvolávať protesty a bude tvrdo bojovať.*[150]

(Ľuboš Blaha, 2021, hereinafter in the section *Metaphorisation of vaccination 2021 in the statuses of Ľuboš Blaha,* examples of Blaha's speech acts are extracted from his vaccination-themed posts published on the Facebook social network from 10 June 2021 to 27 July 2021).[151]

3.1 Referent objects and actors of securitisation

The basic notions of the Copenhagen School's securitisation theory include *referent objects* and *actors of securitisation* (cf. Chapter I). Referent objects are entities that are existentially threatened and can legitimately claim the right to survive. In the utterances (2021) of Ľuboš Blaha, the referent objects threatened by "compulsory vaccination" were traditionally represented by the democratic values of Slovak society, by the social state, by civil rights, public health as well as the health of specific people. In 2023, the key referent objects in Blaha's discourse became democracy, peace, freedom of the media and freedom of expression,

---

150 EL → *The only thing left is the street, riots, blockades, strikes / The explosion will be heard all over Europe / We, as Slovak leftists, will lead the nation in the fight / Smer will call protests during the autumn and fight hard.*

151 Blaha, Ľ. (2021). Facebook. https://www.facebook.com/LBlaha

protection of the traditional family and traditional Slovak values, public and individual health, the lives of Slovaks as well as their human and civil dignity. The main threat to the listed entities in Blaha's interpretation are the current Slovak government, Zuzana Čaputová, the President of the Slovak Republic, NGOs, George Soros as a proper and general name, the EU, NATO, liberals, sun worshippers, the "Ukrainian junta", Bandera's followers and other Russophobes and "fascists" (i.e., in Blaha's rhetoric, all those whose politics and opinions he disagrees with).

A securitisation actor presents a threat as objectively existing for a particular reference object. Thus, the topic is taken out of the ordinary political process and moved to the plane of securitization (through a speech act). As long as the securitisation actor manages to avoid otherwise binding rules and procedures by asserting the priority and urgency of the existential threat to the reference object, we are witnessing an act of successful securitisation.[152] "The influence and position of the securitisation actor in a given society is often crucial for successful securitisation, as his social influence makes the threat become felt as a threat simply by the actor perceiving it as such and stating it publicly."[153] Ľuboš Blaha, undoubtedly a prominent actor in the securitization of (not only) vaccination, but other resonant social topics, is known for his harsh, even hateful language in his social media statuses, where he uncompromisingly declares in the description (motto) of his site: *If you're fed up with right-wing liberals, Russophobes and anti-communists, you're on the right website. This is the site of the most leftist member of the Slovak parliament.* The colloquial phraseme *"mať plné zuby"* (translated as *to be fed up*, literal translation: *to have full teeth*) has distinctly negative connotations in the Slovak linguistic representation of the world and fully captures the essence of the politician's everyday statuses. It is a "linguistic eye-catcher" for dissatisfied citizens and a speech tactic of the popular discourse strategy of populism, "I am one of you – I speak to my people".

3.2 Metaphor as an object of research

Contemporary cognitive linguistics considers metaphor not only a trope and ornament of speech, but also a form of thinking, an important cognitive process, a way of cognition, categorization, conceptualization and evaluation

---

152   Buzan, Wæver, & Wilde, 1998, p. 25.
153   More details in Štefančík, & Dulebová, 2017, p. 53.

of the world.[154] According to Susanne Kirchoff,[155] metaphors contribute to the formation of the identity of a society or a particular linguistic community. In public discourses, they shape patterns of social reasoning and can contribute to the collective construction of reality by creating a shared world within a speech community.

In modern cognitive metaphorology, one of the most prominent approaches to the study of material is the discourse approach, which can also be used in the case of the analysis of the metaphorical articulation of vaccination and other securitized topics. The latter assumes, first of all, the consideration of a number of contextual (linguistic and extralinguistic) factors. According to the distinguished Russian politolinguist Anatoliy Chudinov, "metaphorical models should be studied in discourse, in close connection with the conditions of their emergence and functioning, taking into account the author's intentions and pragmatic characteristics against a broad socio-political background. The system of metaphorical models is an important part of the national linguistic image of the world, the national mentality, it is closely related to the history of the nation and the current socio-political situation."[156]

Contemporary metaphorology also provides important theoretical grounding for research in political linguistics, since "political metaphors serve as important means of reducing political and ideological arguments to simple formulas and interpreting events and developments in the form of polar alternatives."[157]

Metaphor research is also coming to the fore in media linguistics, as the authors of media texts use metaphors to create cognitive attitudes or false stereotypes of thinking in the population that are advantageous to them, to change the value system of recipients, to spread misinformation and to create myths.[158] Traditionally, the most important functions of metaphors in media texts include cognitive, communicative, persuasive, modelling, popularizing, axiological, expressive-evaluative, euphemistic, pragmatic, aesthetic, nominative, explanatory,

---

154   Dulebová, I., & Krajčovičová, L. (2020). Methaphorical image of Brexit in Russian media discourse (based on the methaphor of theatre). *Annales Scientia Politica, 9*(1), 18–28.

155   Kirchhoff, S. (2010). *Krieg mit Methaphern. Mediendiskurse über 9/11 und den „War onTerror"*. Bielefeld: transcript Verlag.

156   Chudinov, 2013, p. 27.

157   Pörksen, B. (2000). *Die Konstruktion von Feindbildern. Zum Sprachgebrauch vonneonazistischen Medien*. Wiesbaden: Westdeutscher Verlag, p. 170.

158   Dulebová, & Krajčovičová, 2020, p. 20.

manipulative and other functions.[159] While analysing metaphorization in the process of vaccination securitizing in the left-wing political discourse, it will be interesting to see which of these emerge at the forefront.

The conflictogenic nature of the analysed metaphors is also important. It can be found mainly in metaphorical models with conceptual vectors of cruelty and aggression (military and criminal metaphors), metaphors articulating deviation from the natural course of things (morbial metaphors), metaphors of material calculation (financial metaphors), zoomorphic and physiological metaphors, metaphors of sport (emphasizing the competitive nature of the event), and occasionally even seemingly constructive metaphors of the family or a building (when pointing to their disintegration, collapse, etc.)[160]

3.3 Metaphorization of 2021 vaccination in FB statuses of Ľuboš Blaha

Based on the excerpted material (selection and systematization of metaphors thematizing vaccination from the statuses of Ľuboš Blaha published from 10 June 2021 to 27 September 2021) and its subsequent content analysis, we present only the most frequent (consistently recurring) metaphorical models (for interpretive analysis) and try to explain the pragmatic intention of their use by the actors of vaccination securitization.

Judging by our observations, in the process of vaccination metaphorization, Blaha, turns to usual or even stereotypical images (referring most often to notorious facts of history); one can also speak of a considerable instrumentalization of history (in favour of the author's intentions), as well as the construction of exceptionally conflictogenic metaphorical concepts.

Clearly the most frequently used conceptual scheme (frame) is *fascism* (which also corresponds to a number of thematically correlated slots such *as Gestapo, concentration camps, Auschwitz, Dr. Mengele*, etc.):

SL → *Táto vláda oficiálne zavádza **fašizmus** / ako kedysi Hitler, treba tlačiť **fašistický naratív**, že ľudia sa delia na elitu a spodinu / liberálni **fašisti** / očkovací **fašista** / vyhráža učiteľom terorom ako posledný **fašista** / pandemický **fašizmus** / očkovací **fašizmus** sa rozlieza po celom svete / nie ste pre nich slobodný človek, vy ste vlastníctvo **fašistického štátu** a ten si s vašim telom môže robiť, čo chce / ak niekto kolaboruje s **fašistami**, pre mňa prestal existovať / v skutočnosti iba **fašizujú** slovenskú spoločnosť / To je tak, keď **fašista***

---

159   Duskayeva, L. a kol. (2018). *Medialingvistika v terminach i ponatiyach. Slovar – spravochnik*. Moskva: Flinta.

160   In more details Dulebová, & Krajčovičová, 2020, p. 21.

kričí, chyťte **fašistu** / *liberálna kaviareň úplne bezstarostne obhajuje* **fašistické** *praktiky, inšpiruje sa diktatúrami / Že sa nehanbia,* **fašisti**! / *Musíme očkovací* **fašizmus** *zastaviť / považujem to za plazivú* **fašizáciu** / *najnovšie je* **fašizmus** *v móde / povinné očkovanie je* **fašistické** *opatrenie.*[161]

The systematic instrumentalisation of history accompanied by the reinterpretation of ideologies, such as the concept of *fascism* precisely defined in terms of political science (which as can be seen in Blaha's discourse, semantically means everything that does not suit him personally and his political intentions, and which is endlessly repeated in completely different contexts from status to status) leads to a slow but certain emptying of its original meaning, de-ideologization and, consequently, to value disorientation in terms of the historical and cultural memory of the young generation of Slovaks.

In hyponymic relation to the term fascism, there are precedent names with extremely strong negative connotations – *Mengele, Hitler, Goebbels* – well known to every Slovak, which Blaha continuously uses to demonize "compulsory vaccination":

SL → *V minulom živote by zrejme podával skalpely* **doktorovi Mengelemu** / *Od čias* **Josefa Mengeleho** *až doposiaľ toto ľudské právo nikto nespochyboval a odrazu – všetko je inak / ako by sa sem vracala nenávisť, ktorá tu od* **Hitlera** *nebola / povinné očkovanie má bližšie k* **Hitlerovi** *než k modernej demokracii / Namiesto* **goebbelsovskej** *propagandy žiadame objektívne informácie a vyzývame k tomu, aby očkovanie bolo dobrovoľné / Správajú sa ako doktor* **Mengele**, *nútia ľudí do medicínskych experimentov / Od* **Adolfa** *sa líšia len v tom, že nie sú rasisti – im je jedno, akej si farby, oni nenávidia všetkých /* **Mengeleho** *pohrobky / povinné očkovanie experimentálnou vakcínou, pripomína* **Josefa Mengeleho** / *nenávisť sa valí na neočkovaných ľudí od vlády, politikov a médií, mám pocit, že žijeme v* **Hitlerovej** *Tretej ríši / Naposledy podľa*

161　EL → This government is officially implementing **fascism** / like Hitler once did, **the fascist narrative** needs to be pushed through so that people are divided into elite and scum / liberal **fascists** / vaccination **fascist** / threatening teachers with terror like the ultimate **fascist** / pandemic **fascism** / vaccination **fascism** is spreading across the world / you are not a free man to them, you are the property of **the fascist state** and it can do what it wants with your body / if someone collaborates with **fascists,** they cease to exist for me / in fact, they only **fascistize** Slovak society / that's when **a fascist** calls, catch **the fascist** / the liberal coffee-drinkers defend **fascist** practices quite carelessly, taking inspiration from dictatorships / They should be ashamed of themselves, the **fascists**! / We need to stop vaccination **fascism** / I see it as creeping **fascisization** / **Fascism** is in vogue lately / Compulsory vaccination is a **fascist** measure.

*krvnej línie rozlišoval **Alfred Rosenberg**, hlavný nacistický ideológ. A teraz Heger s Lengvarským, gratulujem.*[162]

The metaphor of *Gestapo men*, eliciting immediate reactions of fear, is also impressive:

SL → *Matovičovi **gestapáci** si práve odhlasovali očkovací apartheid a ešte si aj zatlieskali, že z polovice Slovákov urobili podľudí / Toto je Mikulec – **gestapák** na pohľadanie! / to sú **gestapácke** nápady / množstvo korporátnych **gestapákov**.*[163]

The image of the *concentration camp* is in no way inferior to that of the *Gestapo men* in evoking horror, but it is questionable if such parallels do not cross all possible ethical boundaries:

SL → *presne ako bachári v **Osvienčime**, keď Židov hnali do plynových komôr / hrkútajú ako dvaja gestapáci v **Osvienčime** / preventívne nás všetkých niekoľko miliónov strčia do **koncentračného tábora** / sa mentálne zasekli dakedy v roku 1943 v **Mauthausene**.*[164]

Other allusions to 20th century fascism are numerous, mostly associated with threats:

SL → *Už len si **zahajlovať**, Lengvarský, Korčok a ostatní **nahnedlí** pravičiari – skončíte tak, ako vaši zvrátení predchodcovia v roku 1945 / Tie mená novodobých **nacistov** si dobre*

---

162   EL → In a past life, he would probably be handing scalpels to **Dr. Mengele** / From the time of **Josef Mengele** until now, no one has questioned this human right, and suddenly – everything has changed / it's as if the hatred that hasn't been here since **Hitler** is returning / compulsory vaccination is closer to **Hitler** than to modern democracy / Instead of **Goebbelsian** propaganda, we are asking for objective information and calling for vaccinations to be voluntary / They behave like **Dr. Mengele**, forcing people into medical experiments / The only difference from **Adolf** is that they are not racist – they don't care what colour you are, they hate everybody / **Mengele**'s descendants / Compulsory vaccination with an experimental vaccine, reminiscent of **Josef Mengele** / The hatred is pouring in on unvaccinated people from the government, politicians and the media, I feel like we are living in **Hitler's** Third Reich / The last to distinguish by bloodline was **Alfred Rosenberg**, the Nazi's chief ideologue. And now Heger with Lengvarsky are doing it, congratulations.

163   EL → the Matovič **Gestapo** have just voted for vaccination apartheid and even applauded themselves for making untermenschen out of half of the Slovaks / This is Mikulec – a **Gestapo** man to behold! / these are **Gestapo** ideas / lots of corporate **Gestapo** people.

164   SL → just like the guards at **Auschwitz** when they herded Jews into the gas chambers / they cackle like the two Gestapo men at **Auschwitz** / they preventively shove all of us, a few million, into **a concentration camp** / they got mentally stuck in **Mauthausen** sometime in 1943.

zapamätajte – sú to mená, ktoré sa zapíšu do slovenských dejín tak, ako **Alexander Mach** *či* **Vojtech Tuka.** *Tými najtemnejšími písmenami.*[165]

The metaphor of *terror* is also a military metaphor (always conflictogenic):

SL → *Prečo práve teraz* **terorizujú** *ľudí covid-pasmi? / musíme zastaviť očkovací* **teror** */ chcú nás takto* **terorizovať,** *aby sme utekali nechať si pichnúť Pfizer / v armáde idú spustiť čistky a očkovací* **teror.**[166]

(even though the metaphor of *terror* is partially lexicalized in Slovak, in the given context it still retains its expressive charge). For the sake of objectivity, however, we must add that "the metaphor of war is, after all, a natural part of the politicians' manner of expressing themselves, not only across countries, but across time periods as well. Be it in former centuries or at present, for some politicians, politics was and still is associated with the context of war."[167] As a result, the discourse acquires an extremely aggressive dimension which makes it inseparable from the securitization process.

Nevertheless, other historical allusions selected by Blaha for the purpose of securitization have an extremely aggressive colouring and can be summarized in one of his sentences, in which he keeps repeating the same idea over and over again and constructs a negative image of vaccination:

SL → *Tento istý princíp voči Židom uplatňoval* **nacizmus,** *voči Afričanom juhoafrický režim* **apartheidu,** *voči* **otrokom** *režim v USA.*[168]

Thus, in addition to the references to fascism, he continually draws parallels with slavery and apartheid, with the apartheid metaphor prevailing in terms of both quantity and broader contextual engagement:

SL → *majú tam svojich ľudí, ktorí* **zotročia** *Slovensko / pretože nás chcú* **zotročiť** */ po desivých skúsenostiach z 20. storočia s* **apartheidom** *v Južnej Afrike či segregáciou v USA,*

---

165 EL → All that is left to do is **to heil**, Lengvarský, Korčok and the rest of **the brownish rightists** – you will end up like your perverted predecessors in 1945 / Remember well the names of the modern **Nazis** – they are the names that will go down in Slovak history like **Alexander Mach** and **Vojtech Tuka**. In the darkest letters.

166 EL → Why are they **terrorizing** people because of covid-passports right now? / we need to stop vaccination **terror** / they want to **terrorize** us like this so that we run to get Pfizer jabs / they're going to start persecution and vaccination **terror** in the army.

167 Štefančík, R. (2020). Metafora vojny v jazyku politiky. *Lingua et Vita, 17*, 59–69.

168 EL → This same principle was applied against Jews by the **Nazis**, against Africans by the **apartheid** regime in South Africa, against **slaves** by the regime in the U.S.

*dnes hovoriť o občanoch dvoch kategórií / ponechávajú **apartheid** pre neočkovaných.
Nadľudia, podľudia, segregácia / paralely s juhoafrickým **apartheidom**. Najskôr Afričanov
nepustili do reštaurácií či do mesta / prioritou je teraz boj proti očkovaciemu **apartheidu**
/ Čaputovej trvalo až jeden deň, kým podpísala zákon o **očkovacom** apartheide / Pfizer
nie je spása, **apartheid** nie je cesta / Držím palce každému, kto bojuje proti **apartheidu**
/ Učebnicový **apartheid** / Oni tu zavádzajú takú diskrimináciu, akú nemali ani v Južnej
Afrike počas **apartheidu** / Ľudia nechcú **apartheid** – ani tí očkovaní / V reštauráciách,
kde podporujú **apartheid** / Presne toto robme tým, čo kolaborujú so systémom **apartheidu**
/ Už začal platiť režim **apartheidu** a hoci covid môžu roznášať očkovaní aj neočkovaní /
Apartheid sa prehlbuje .*[169]

The second approach (in terms of metaphor frequency) was the tendency to
oversimplify the issue of vaccination, i.e., to narrow the topic to the position
of "pharmaceutical companies as the main evil" (with an emphasis on their
profiteering) and the constant stigmatization of Pfizer as a symbol of all of the
pharmaceutical companies (metonymic transfer):

SL → *Čaputová je **maskot Pfizeru** / si to vymysleli naši fantastickí **farma-liberáli** / Ale
čo čakáte od obrovských **farmaceutických molochov**, ktorým nikdy nešlo o zdravie, ale len
o zisk / stoja pevne v jednom šíku s kaviarňou a **farmafirmami** / Čaputová v OSN robí
kampaň Pfizeru a ospevuje očkovanie / Ona je ako taký **Jukebox farmafiriem** – hodíš do
nej mincu a ona ti odrapká, že vakcína je úsmev / robiť ľudom zo života peklo, ak neurobia
kšeft americkej farmafirme / Lengvarský verne **slúži Pfizeru** ako miestny Vakcinátor /
farma-hrdinovia / To je tak, keď všade len chodíš ako **reklamný transparent Pfizeru**
a bez oponentúry vrieskaš, že vakcína je úsmev / za tie miliardové zisky amerických
farmafiriem to stojí / **Ministerstva Pfizeru** Slovenskej republiky / Slovenská vláda sa
dlhodobo správa ako **marketingové oddelenie Pfizeru** / **rozkaz Pfizeru** "znel jasne" /*

---

169   EL → they have their people there who will **enslave** Slovakia / because they wish
to **enslave** us / after the horrific 20th century experiences of **apartheid** in South
Africa or segregation in the USA, to talk about two categories of citizens today /
they leave **apartheid** for the unvaccinated. Superhumans, subhumans, segregation
/ parallels with South African **apartheid**. First, Africans weren't allowed into
restaurants or town / the priority now is to fight vaccination **apartheid** / Čaputová
took no more than a day to sign the **vaccination apartheid** act into law / Pfizer is
not salvation, **apartheid** is not the way / My fingers are crossed for anyone who
fights **apartheid** / Textbook example of **apartheid** / They are introducing the kind
of discrimination here that didn't even exist in South Africa during **apartheid**
/ People don't want **apartheid** – not even the vaccinated ones / In restaurants
where they support **apartheid** / This is exactly what we should do to those who
collaborate with the **apartheid** system / The **apartheid** regime is already in place
and although covid can be spread by both the vaccinated and the unvaccinated /
Apartheid is deepening.

správate sa ako reklamný maskot Pfizeru / kľúčenka od Pfizeru / naša Pfizer-vláda a jej skorumpovaná tlač.[170]

As can be seen, the metaphorical projection is primarily directed at the potentially huge profits of the pharmaceutical companies (which is, after all, symptomatic of the rhetoric of any leftist) in order to induce a sense of social inferiority and financial injustice in their supporters, as well as to articulate the alleged "dependence" of the current government, the media and, in particular, President Čaputová on pharmaceutical companies, claiming that they also profit from it (without evidence on the factual level, but solely on the level of the persuasive speech acts mentioned above).

The third most widespread tendency in the process of vaccination securitization was the metaphorical use of the conceptual scheme of *science* (in other contexts largely non-conflicted) with its corresponding slots of *laboratory, medical experiments*. Blaha's discursive intention is explicit and easy to achieve, namely, to induce fear of a possible threat to health, since these concepts (*laboratory, experiment*) have connotations not only of scientific progress, but also of an often unpredictable, uncertain outcome. The speech tactics logically correspond to this strategy:

SL → *premenujme Slovenskú republiku na **Slovenské laboratórium** / sme len **laboratórium** pre americké farmafirmy / kým ich neodstavíme od moci, Slovensko bude **americké laboratórium** / Už dnes nás premenili na **laboratórium**. Slovensko je jediná krajina, kde prebiehajú experimenty Pfizeru s očkovaním detí / naše 5-ročné deti obetujú pre klinickú štúdiu Pfizeru. Medicínsky sme sa stali **laboratóriom** pre ich očkovacie pokusy / oberajú tých najslabších o poslednú kôrku chleba, ale ešte aj idú robiť **medicínske experimenty***

---

170   EL → Čaputová is the **mascot of Pfizer** / invented by our fantastic **pharma-liberals** / But what do you expect from giant **pharmaceutical molochs** who never cared about health, just about profit / they're firmly in lockstep with the coffee-drinkers (derogatory, referring to liberal intellectuals, author's note) and the **pharmaceutical companies** / at the UN, Čaputová is **campaigning for Pfizer** and glorifying vaccination / she's like some **jukebox for the pharmaceuticals** – you throw a coin at her and she'll tell you the vaccine is a smile / making people's lives a living hell, if they don't do **business for the American pharma** / Lengvarský loyally **serves Pfizer** as a local vaccinator / **pharma-heroes** / It's like that when you go around like a **Pfizer advertising banner** and without opposition scream that the vaccine is a smile / it's worth the billion-dollar profits of the **American pharmaceuticals** / the **Pfizer Ministry of the Slovak Republic** / the Slovak government has long behaved like a **Pfizer marketing department** / **Pfizer's command** "sounded clear" / you behave like a **Pfizer advertising mascot** / a **Pfizer key tag** / our **Pfizer-government** and its corrupt press.

na našich malých deťoch / Na slovenských deťoch idú **páchať medicínsky experiment** */ V Afrike už ich nechcú, tak zjavne svoje* **pokusy** *na deťoch presunuli na Slovensko.*[171]

In an effort to approach his audience, Blaha often turns to colloquial phrasemes:

SL → *rehlí ako lečo/robiť zo života peklo/jedna babka povedala/sa boja ľudí ako čert kríža/ dajte preč paprče/sa môžete rozkrájať aj na franforce/mastí vačky Pfizeru.*[172]

and occasionally we find phrasemes and precedent expressions in a transformed version (*where did the comrades from Pfizer go wrong*[173]) which correspond to his intentions and functions as a source of expressiveness and pun, which is met with an exceptionally favourable response from the recipient (in more detail Gajarský, Iermachkova, Spišiaková 2021)[174].

Apart from lexicalized metaphors ("*experimental rabbits*", "*dirty game*"), in the statuses of Blaha thematizing vaccination, we can often encounter hyperbolization:

SL → *zločin proti ľudskosti, bezbrehá vakcinačná ideológia, neoliberálne monštrá, vláda smrti, najväčší politický súboj našich čias, krvavé ruky.*[175]

Interestingly, he occasionally turns to Slovak linguaculturemes, but also to universally-precedented phenomena of literary origin in the process of metaphorization, using more often references to basic works (often of a fairy-tale

---

171 EL → Let's rename the Slovak Republic to **Slovak Laboratory** / we are just a **laboratory** for American pharmaceuticals / until we remove them from power, Slovakia will be an **American laboratory** / They have already turned us into a **laboratory**. Slovakia is the only country where the Pfizer experiments with the vaccination of children are going on / our 5-year-old children are being sacrificed to Pfizer's clinical trial. Medically we have become a **laboratory** for their vaccination experiments / they are robbing the weakest of the last piece of bread, but they are even going to do **medical experiments** on our little children / they are going to **commit a medical experiment** on Slovak children / in Africa they don't want them anymore, so apparently, they have moved their **experiments** to children to Slovakia.

172 EL → laughs like a drain, make life a living hell, one granny said, be scared of people like the devil fears the cross, take your hands off, you can tear yourself to shreds (literal translation of an idiom, meaning: no matter what you do, author's note), helps Pfizer make lots of money.

173 A modified precedent expression from the film entitled *Pelíšky* (Jan Hřebejk, 1999).

174 Gajarský, L., Iermačková, O., & Spišiaková, A. (2021). Transformations of phraseological units in Russian and Slovak advertising slogans. *Filologičeskije nauki, 4*, 11–17.

175 EL → crime against humanity, mindless vaccination ideology, neoliberal monsters, reign of death, the greatest political battle of our time, bloodied hands.

and folklore nature), generally well known to all representatives of the Slovak linguacultural community:

> SL → *Keby ešte žil* **Pavol Dobšinský**, *tak by určite začal zbierať všetky rozprávky o očkovaní, ktoré na nás chrlí naša Pfizer-vláda a jej skorumpovaná tlač / Raz tie ich rozprávky zozbierame do knihy* **Tisíc a jedna dávka**. *A bude z toho hit / Slovensko* **farmadrakom zotne** *všetky* **hlavy**.[176]

Blaha also employs appellativization (changing a proper name to a generic one), for example, the name of the famous Slovak humorist Jozef Pročko, as a personification of all the negative characteristics of the current coalition politicians arguing for the meaningfulness of vaccination:

> SL → *Oni sú hlúpejší ako ten planktón. Neexistuje primitívnejšia forma existencie ako* **pročkovia** *v slovenskom parlamente /* *Koaliční* **pročkovia** *zarezali všetky naše mimoriadne schôdze / rôzni primitívni* **pročkovia** */ parlamentní* **pročkovia**.[177]

However, the frequent repetition of a given appellative reduces its intended ironic expressive effect.

Unusual for the discursive tactics of a leftist radical are metaphorical references ironizing representatives or symbols of communist ideology:

> SL → *Liberáli to dávajú na* **Gottwalda** */ tu bude ako v* **Severnej Kórei** */ sú tu také zákazy, že by aj* **aparátčici za bývalého režimu** *mohli závidieť / ubijú ľudí* **severokórejskou propagandou** *a ani len nepripustia vyváženejšiu diskusiu o očkovaní.*[178]

In the creation of metaphors (as we have already pointed out) Blaha is considerably redundant, which is particularly noticeable in the area of the so-called developed metaphors, which in the case of repetition (even with a distance of several days) can sound almost intrusive to an attentive reader:

---

176   EL → If **Pavol Dobšinský** were still alive, he would surely start collecting all the tales about vaccination that our Pfizer-government and its corrupt press spew at us / One day we will collect those tales into a book called **A Thousand and One Doses**. And it'll be a hit / Slovakia will **cut off the heads of** all the **pharmadragons**.

177   EL → They're dumber than plankton. There is no more primitive form of existence than the **pročkos** in the Slovak parliament / Coalition **pročkos** have cut all our special sessions / various primitive **pročkos** / parliamentary **pročkos**.

178   EL → Liberals are playing it like **Gottwald** / it's going to be like **North Korea** here / there are bans that would make even **apparatchiks of the former regime** jealous / they're going to hammer people with **North Korean propaganda** and won't even allow a more balanced discussion about vaccination.

SL → *Farmafirmy sa budú topiť v prachoch a ľudia budú napichaní zhruba **ako priemerný** **feťák z Ovsišťa** / Vraždia demokraciu v priamom prenose. Ľudia budú na včeličku behať každý deň **ako priemerný feťák z Ovsišťa**.*[179]

We also observe attempts at word formation on a metaphorical basis, but the occasionalism *Vaccinistan* (*We are Vaccinistan*) has not yet taken hold in Slovak political discourse. Blaha is also particularly fond of metaphorising potential social unrest (*boiling, explosion, pressure cooker*):

SL → *V Slovákoch to **vrie** ako nikdy. Však provokujte ďalej – len potom neplačte, keď to **vybuchne**, liberálni fašisti! / **tlakový hrniec** je natlakovaný ako nikdy / Toto bude **najhorúcejšia** jeseň v našich dejinách.*[180]

Even though the threats did not materialize in the end, the securitization can be considered successful (completed), as it helped to trigger public pressure to hold a referendum on pre-term elections (which finally took place on January 21, 2023 and was unsuccessful).

The topic of vaccination in Blaha's statuses acquires an emotional (especially ironic and judgmental) colouring through metaphorization. Moreover, it exhibits a distinctly conflictogenic vector directed towards its stigmatization and subsequent securitization. The author makes sophisticated use of emotionally-coloured expressions, metaphors, hyperboles, substandard lexis (sociolects, jargonisms and vulgarisms) with the intention of convincing the public of the danger of vaccination, which, in his opinion, becomes a threat to such abstract endangered entities (reference objects) as the civil rights of human beings, democratic values, the rule of law, the welfare state and the equality of citizens.

In the case of the securitization of "compulsory vaccination", as a "linguistic litmus test", the prevalence of conflictogenic metaphors would point to a negative semantic projection of the event in question, and its modelling in the consciousness of the recipient as harmful, reprehensible and dangerous.

In in the process of the securitization of vaccination in Blaha's statuses, the established dominant ideologemes or more narrowly perceived politemes of public discourse (power, state, politics, ideology, government, parliament,

---

179   EL → The pharma companies will be drowning in cash and people will be stoned **like the average junkie from Ovsište** / They are slaughtering democracy live on air. People will be rushing to get the "bee" every day **like an average junkie from Ovsište**.

180   EL → It's **boiling** like never before in Slovak souls. Go on provoking – but don't cry when it **explodes,** liberal fascists! / The **pressure cooker** is pressurized as never before / This is going to be **the hottest** autumn in our history.

political party, etc.[181] acquire new connotations and thus a new axiological dimension, which can lead to a change in the nature of political discourse and deepen the crisis of values that is manifested today in various areas of social life.

Our analysis of the prevailing functions of metaphors in Blaha's statuses securitizing vaccination suggests that the key functions in a particular case include persuasive, axiological, expressive and modelling functions. Although the expressive function comes to the fore externally, equally important is the modelling function, which shapes ideas about vaccination in the form of a model that demonizes the very notion of vaccines in every aspect. The persuasive function manifests itself in an attempt to influence the addressee and induce a sense of impending danger, and the axiological function in creating in the recipient a system of values favourable to the actor of securitization (through an unambiguous and unidirectional figurative evaluation). Metaphorical statements affect not so much the logical as the emotional side of perception. The online space itself "as a communicative field of emotions [...], in which it seems to be a kind of extra requirement to insist on reasoned judgments based on a rational consideration of context where a fragment, a photo, a thumbs up (like), a thumbs down (hate), an emoticon, or an emoji [...] is expected, helps to do so. The architecture of online communities is based on emotionality, not rationality; by their very nature they create space for making up stories, for various constructions without a factual basis, for passing off the imaginary as real, in short, for creating an arena of fabrications."[182]

Although the peculiarities of the idiolect of Ľuboš Blaha, the vice-president of the Smer-SD political party (a prominent actor of securitization) is only a secondary subject of our research, based on the analysis of his Facebook statuses shared from June to September 2021, we can conclude that despite his reputation as an experienced demagogue and orator, he is considerably monothematic; he repeatedly uses the same metaphors and hyperboles and is linguistically unimaginative and synonymically uncreative. His speech acts are predominantly colloquial in nature and full of substandard lexis and vulgarisms. His securitizing statuses are characterized by tautology, pleonasms and redundancy, although

---

181 Molnárová, E. (2013). *Spoločensko-politická lexika z kontrastívneho aspektu*. Banská Bystrica: Belianum, FHV UMB, p. 8.

182 Sámelová, A. (2020). Online komunity ako producenti mediálnych obsahov. In A. Sámelová, M. Stanková, & J. Hacek, J. (Eds.), *Fenomén 2020: komunita v mediálnom priestore* (pp. 18–26). Bratislava: Univerzita Komenského v Bratislave.

they can also be seen as deliberate speech tactics corresponding to his intentions to influence the target audience, after all, repetitio est mater studiorum, and the method of multiple repetitions is even recommended as one of the basic practices in pedagogy. From a linguistic point of view, continuous repetition can also be seen as deliberately created stylistic figures (anaphora, epiphora, epizeuxis, anadiplosis, parallelism, etc.), but then we should also see the texts of his statuses as works of art. However, arguably, the extraordinary speed of production of the analysed texts (at least one per day, but often at intervals of several hours) does not allow them to go beyond the colloquial style (in written form), which is, after all, characteristic of most Facebook statuses. It is essential to induce fear, to create a sense of threat, and in this case for political populists in the information war that is gaining momentum in Slovakia and elsewhere in the spirit of Machiavellianism – "the end justifies the means".

3.4 Ľuboš Blaha's securitization strategies and speech tactics in the 2023 election year

Ľuboš Blaha has consistently and continuously proceeded in creating a sense of constant threat and undermining confidence in the current pro-European direction of Slovak politics, with the difference that he has transferred his securitization activities to the Russian Telegram network, the essence of which was aptly described by RTVS editor Miroslava Hospodárová on 23 March 2022: "The Russian social network Telegram is a haven for Slovak disinformation sites: the blocking of disinformation sites and the threat of prosecution for approving the Russian invasion of Ukraine are changing the internet in Slovakia and the Czech Republic. Disinformation websites are moving their headquarters abroad and some have moved to lesser-known networks in Slovakia, such as Telegram. It is neither a social network nor a chat platform. Experts consider it an information hybrid. The latest analysis shows that in Slovakia and the Czech Republic similar networks have become a haven for conspirators, especially their hard core. A large amount of malicious material has started to appear there. It can be said that there was illegal content too, which was disseminated to a large number of users."[183]

---

183   Rozhlas a televízia Slovenska (2022, March 23). Ruská sociálna sieť Telegram je útočiskom pre slovenské dezinformačné weby. *RTVS*. https://spravy.rtvs.sk/2022/03/ruska-socialna-siet-telegram-je-utociskom-pre-slovenske-dezinformacne-weby/

In the light of these facts, it is not surprising that Blaha shifted his manipulative securitization activities to the aforementioned network, and therefore all the following examples of his speech acts are excerpted from the freely available channel in Telegram.[184] He has 34 thousand official followers there, which does not indicate the real number of viewers at all, since the channel is publicly accessible and there is nothing to prevent interested viewers from following it "unregistered".

He likes to draw public attention to the success of his Telegram channel, and does not hide the fact that his controversial views are the main reason behind it:

> SL → Už nás objavili aj v českých liberálnych médiách: **Vyplakávajú**, že ľudia masovo opúšťajú Facebook, kde pritvrdzujú cenzori a prechádzajú na Telegram. A vraj na Slovensku je Telegram oveľa silnejší ako v Česku, čo dokladujú úspechmi Dannyho Kollára a Ľuboša Blahu. Aha, čo o nás **česká pobočka americkej propagandy** píše: "Vlivný je také místopředseda strany Smer Ľuboš Blaha, který propaguje kremelskou verzi o válce na Ukrajině. Za viníka invaze označuje Západ a Ukrajince, ukrajinský prezident Volodymyr Zelenskyj chce podle něj rozeštvat Evropu." Klasika – ak chceš mier, tak si ruský agent. Už tomu chýbajú iba **vreskoty amerických uletencov**, že chcieť mier, to je ako **pomáhať Hitlerovi**. Aj takéto **retardované reakcie** občas počúvame.[185]

His securitization strategies have changed in respect of reference objects in 2023 (compared to 2021), as the issue of vaccinations is no longer "socially urgent"; however, the hate speech communication tactics remain the same. Colloquial, vulgar and insulting language is commonplace (moaning, screams of misfits, retarded reactions). He repeatedly refers to negative historical precedents (Hitler), emphasizes that propaganda is always American and repeats his denial of connections to Kremlin propaganda (Russian agent).

Among the threatened entities (referential objects), space is given to the abstract notion of *democracy* (which is embodied, as can be expected, exclusively by the populist left-wing party SMER), threats to *media freedom and freedom of*

---

184   Blaha, Ľ. (2023, April). Telegram. https://t.me/s/LubosBlahaSmer

185   EL → *The Czech liberal media have already discovered us: **they are moaning** that people are leaving Facebook en masse, where the censors are tightening their grip, and switching to Telegram. And they say that Telegram is much stronger in Slovakia than in the Czech Republic, which they prove by referring to the success of Danny Kollár and Ľuboš Blaha. Look at what **the Czech branch of American propaganda** writes about us: "Ľuboš Blaha, vice-chairman of the Smer party, is also influential, promoting the Kremlin's version of the war in Ukraine. He blames the West and Ukrainians for the invasion and says Ukrainian President Volodymyr Zelensky wants to disintegrate Europe." Classics – if you want peace, you're a Russian agent. What's missing here are just **the screams of American misfits** that wanting peace is like **helping Hitler**. We hear such **retarded reactions** from time to time too.*

expression, to peace, human and civil dignity, traditional family and traditional Slovak values, human life, public health, etc.

The announcement of pre-term parliamentary elections (30 September 2023) is proof of successful securitization by the Slovak political opposition (primarily SMER representatives) in 2020–2023, and in the pre-election struggle that is gaining momentum, all discursive political strategies are being used (mostly with the vector of intimidation), including lies, disinformation, conspiracy claims and the distortion of facts. But regarding what is essential for our research (focused on the lexical level of language) all of the aforementioned manipulative strategies are primarily implemented through emotionally appealing speech acts with a strong negative connotation.

Threats to democracy. What are the major threats to democracy in Slovakia today, according to the Telegram channel[186] and what linguistic means help to highlight this threat? The graphic form of the original is preserved, namely the deliberate use of capital letters in order to emphasize the idea in the subtitle of each post:

SL → *LIBERÁLI UŽ VO SVOJICH ÚTOKOCH NA DEMOKRACIU PREKONÁVAJÚ AJ FAŠISTOV: Obhajujú kriminalizáciu iných názorov, čo je typický znak každého fašizmu. Obhajujú likvidáciu opozičných médií. Presne ako fašisti. Obhajujú zneužívanie trestného práva na lynčovanie opozície. Aj túto disciplínu mimoriadne obľuboval istý Adolf Há. Bravó, aké je ľahké prepracovať sa za pár rokov od liberalizmu k fašizmu. Ešte aj oprášili starý fašistický pozdrav Sláva Ukrajine. Ale v jednej veci sa novodobým liberálom podarilo zájsť ešte ďalej ako fašisti. Fašisti sa snažili dostať masy na svoju stranu, no liberáli ľuďmi až tak veľmi pohŕdajú, že väčšinu národa označia za dezolátov a vyhlása, že sú hrozba. Takúto aroganciu si nedovolil ani Benito vo svojich najtotalitnejších chvíľach. Oni neuveriteľne uleteli – obhajujú číru totalitu. A vraj "liberáli" (1.6.2023).*[187]

---

186   Blaha, Ľ. (2023). Telegram. https://t.me/s/LubosBlahaSmer

187   EL → *LIBERALS HAVE ALREADY COME TO SURPASS **FASCISTS** IN THEIR ATTACKS ON DEMOCRACY: They advocate criminalizing dissenting views, which is a typical feature of all forms of **fascism**. They advocate the elimination of opposition media. Just like **fascists**. They advocate the abuse of criminal law **to lynch** the opposition. A certain **Adolf H.** was immensely fond of this discipline as well. Bravo, how easy it is to go from liberalism to **fascism** in just a few years. They have even dusted off the old **fascist salute** Glory to Ukraine. But in one respect, the modern-times liberals managed to go **even further than fascists**. Fascists tried to get the nation on their side, but liberals despise the people so much that they label most of the populace as degenerates and declare them a threat. Not even **Benito** in his most totalitarian moments dared such arrogance. They have flown off the handle unbelievably – they advocate sheer totalitarianism. And they say they are "liberals" (1.6.2023).*

As we can see, in one short post, *liberals* (the main threat to democracy in Slovakia according to Blaha) are compared to fascism or to precedent names symbolizing fascism (Adolf Ha, Benito) 9 times. The ideologeme of fascism is re-semanticized and operates in the discourse of the securitization actor as a pejorative lexical means. As in the case of the securitization of vaccination, the pejorative metaphors of *lynching* or *criminalization* are used to instrumentalize and distort history (*the fascist salute Glory to Ukraine*). In this historical aspect, it is remarkable that an admirer of Marxist theories and a leftist who nostalgically idealizes the socialist period (the Czechoslovak Socialist Republic) uncritically applies the concept of totalitarianism exclusively to the current political situation as a characteristic of the liberals' activity (*they advocate sheer totalitarianism*), yet deliberately "forgets" about the experience of the sad history of the 20th century, which demonstrated the dimensions of totalitarianism based on communist ideology. No matter what, Blaha consistently defends socialist totalitarianism:

> SL → **Liberálni zlodeji** teraz kričia, akí boli komunisti zlí a ako naše mamy a otcovia premárnili život v socializme. Že ich **hanba nefacká**. (1.05.2023)[188]

According to Blaha, the main "nominal" threat to democracy in Slovakia is the liberal president Čaputová, whose name he redundantly, even obsessively, associates with the name of George Soros:

> SL → *ČAPUTOVÁ **VYHLÁSILA VOJNU** SLOVENSKU – MY HO NAĎALEJ BUDEME BRÁNIŤ: Po dnešku sa Slovensko rozdelilo na dva tábory. Tábor Zuzany Čaputovej a tábor Roberta Fica. Druhý tábor na čele s nami sa postavil proti Čaputovej vláde, ktorá je nielenže **nedemokratická, neoliberálna a protislovenská**, ale na premiérskom poste navyše bude stáť **Sorosov človek**. Ako je možné, že na čelo svojej vlády postavila zamestnanca **Sorosovej univerzity** magistra Ódora? Dlhých 16 rokov bola pani Čaputová aktivistkou vo Via Iuris, ktorú financovala **Sorosova nadácia** – je náhoda, že dnes bude na čele jej vlády **Sorosov človek?** Pýtame sa, ako si prezidentka môže dovoliť **ignorovať základné piliere** parlamentnej **demokracie** a skladať si vládu bez konzultácií s parlamentom? Kľúčovou témou volieb bude – ste **za čaputovskú beznádej? Za dúhu, voľný trh, Sorosa a vojnu?** Alebo ste za Roberta Fica a národnú ľavicu? Za suverenitu? Za mier? Prosím, nenechajme liberálne mimovládky, aby **ukradli** naše krásne Slovensko – blíži sa rozhodujúci **zápas** našich moderných dejín. (10.5.2023) / K MOCI SA **DERIE SOROSOVA VLÁDA**: predseda Čaputovej vlády, magister Ódor je **Sorosov človek**. Pracuje na Stredoeurópskej univerzite, ktorú **financuje Soros**. Takzvaná úradnícka vláda ... bude to **sorosovsko**-matovičovská*

---

188   EL → **Liberal thieves** are now yelling about how evil the communists were and how our mothers and fathers wasted their lives under socialism. They **should be ashamed** (neutral translation of an expressive Slovak idiom). (1.05.2023)

*banda. Na tlačovke som vecne a faktograficky pripomenul, čo je zač **George Soros** a ako je prepojený so Zuzanou Čaputovou... Dejú sa strašné veci – berú nám demokraciu, berú nám Slovensko. Ďalší **neoliberálny majdan** (9.05.2023).*[189]

As can be seen, the name of George Soros in Blaha's securitization discourse is repeated as a mantra, an incantation, and as a concept it reaches almost unlimited semantic range and extraordinary variability of connections. As a signature anthroponym and pejorative figure of speech, the use of the name Soros is symptomatic of the entire Slovak political discourse (of conspiratory, radical, populist orientation), and we can also observe the completion of the process of appellativization (when a proper name becomes a generic name, a symbol) of the name Soros in the Slovak linguistic representation of the world. This is also observed in the opinion forming newspaper Denník N[190]:

---

189 EL → ČAPUTOVÁ HAS **DECLARED WAR** ON SLOVAKIA – WE WILL CONTINUE DEFENDING IT: After this day, Slovakia is divided into two camps. The camp of Zuzana Čaputová and the camp of Robert Fico. The second camp, led by us, opposes the Čaputová government, which is not only **undemocratic, neoliberal and anti-Slovak,** but it will also have a **Soros man** in the position of Prime Minister. How come she put a **Soros University** employee, Master Ódor, at the head of her government? For 16 long years, Mrs Čaputová was an activist in Via Iuris, which was funded by the **Soros Foundation** – is it a coincidence that today her government will be headed by **a Soros man**? We are asking, how can the President afford to **ignore the basic pillars** of parliamentary **democracy** and create her government without consulting the parliament? The key issue of the elections will be – do you stand for **hopelessness – Čaputová style? For the rainbow, the free market, Soros and war?** Or are you for Robert Fico and the national left? For sovereignty? For peace? Please, do not let the liberal NGOs steal our beautiful Slovakia – the decisive battle of our modern history is approaching. (10 May 2023) / **SOROS GOVERNMENT PUSHING TOWARDS POWER**: the Prime Minister of Čaputova's government, M.A. Ódor is a **Soros man**. He works at the Central European University, which is **funded by Soros**. The so-called bureaucratic government ... it's gonna be a **Soros**-Matovič **gang**. At the press conference, I matter-of-factly and to the point reminded them who **George Soros** was and how he was connected to Zuzana Čaputová ... Terrible things are happening – they are taking away our democracy, they are taking away Slovakia. Another **neoliberal maidan**.(9 May 2023)

190 Denník N. (2023). *Denník N.* https://dennikn.sk/minuta/3380954

SL → *To, ako Robert Fico spomína Georga Sorosa, je podľa sociológa Michala Vašečku prekročením všetkých čiar. „Moje kolegyne urobili krátku analýzu. Robert Fico to vypustí a jeden týždeň sa na facebooku deje toto: „Sorosova bábka, Sorosova nevesta, Sorosova šéfka, Sorosova ovca, Sorosovo decko, Sorosov produkt, Sorosova pracovníčka, Sorosov trójsky kôň, miss Soros…"*[191]

The metaphorical concept of war (*Čaputová has declared war on Slovakia – we will continue defending it*) is used with the explicit intention of reinforcing his own positive image of the only unbreakable defender of the homeland and creating a sense of threat in the recipient. The same intention (of threat) is behind the metaphor of *Maidan*, which is favoured by pro-Russian populists as a symbol of political chaos, coup d'état and social uncertainties.

The threat to freedom of the media and freedom of expression is actually an effort on the part of state institutions to prevent the spread of disinformation and conspiracy theories in so called alternative media, such as *Zem a Vek, Slobodný vysielač and Hlavné správy*, which Blaha cites as examples of independent free media and glorifies in every possible way, as opposed to the "corrupt, manipulative" liberal media. In doing so, he places himself in the position of a victim:

SL → *Do vládnej RTVS ma* **nepustia**, *v súkromných médiách* **ma milionári zakázali**, *z amerického Facebooku ma na žiadosť Čaputovej zamestnanca* **vyhodili**… (25.04.2023).[192]

A well-planned gradation, because compassion for a person who is *not allowed* anywhere, *banned, kicked out*, is guaranteed, and hence the rise of protest moods and one's own preferences. Public, liberal and mainstream media are thus a major threat to freedom of speech because they *bully, criminalize, kick, devastate, censor, and cross all boundaries*:

SL → *LIBERÁLNE MÉDIÁ* **NA HULVÁTA** *ŠÍRIA KONŠPIRAČNÉ TEÓRIE: Slovenské korporátne médiá sa* **prepadajú do takej stoky, že už neexistuje dno, ktoré by ešte neprerazili**. *To ani v Severnej Kórei to* **nedávajú takto na hulváta**. *A televízie? To, čo* **páchajú**, *je vrchol arogancie. Do RTVS nepozvú nikoho z opozície –* **hrkútajú** *si tam Šeliga*

---

191   EL → According to sociologist Michal Vašečka, the way Robert Fico mentions George Soros crosses all lines. "My colleagues did a short analysis. Robert Fico lets it out and for a week this is what happens on Facebook: "Soros puppet, Soros bride, Soros boss, Soros sheep, Soros kid, Soros product, Soros worker, Soros Trojan horse, Miss Soros…"

192   EL → **I will not be allowed** in the government-run RTVS, **I have been banned** from private **media by millionaires**, **I have been kicked out** of the American Facebook at the request of a Čaputová employee… (25 April 2023).

*s Gröhlingom. Dvaja **fušeri**, čo Matovičovi a Sulíkovi tri roky asistovali pri **devastácii** Slovenska. Kovačič na Markíze **kopal do Roba Kaliňáka ako zmyslov zbavený**. Neustále prerušovanie, skákanie do reči, **level krčmy v piatok po polnoci**. Mediálnu sféru ovládla **slniečkarska extrémistická mládež** bez vzdelania a morálky. Amerika, liberalizmus, rusofóbia a nenávisť voči Smeru – toto je ich mentálny horizont (29.05.2023) / ÉRA AMERIKY KONČÍ – PRETO SA NÁS TAK BOJA: Včera oslavoval 10. výročie časopis Zem a vek. Bolo mi cťou, že som mohol vystúpiť a zablahoželať Tiborovi Rostasovi k jeho úspešnému projektu. Alternatíve sa podarilo jedno. **Boja sa nás.** Inak by nás neprenasledovali, inak by nás nekriminalizovali. Najnovšie majú nový cenzorský orgán – Mediálnu radu. Tá **šikanuje** už aj alternatívne médiá. Dírer či Závodský môžu **šíriť svoju slniečkarsku propagandu**, ale Zem a vek či Slobodný vysielač nesmie dať priestor iným názorom. **Dvojaký kilometer.** Mediálna rada sa stáva systémovým **ohrozením slobody slova. Režimová **ideopolícia. Gestapo.** Po voľbách bude treba urobiť poriadok – cenzori v demokracii nemajú čo hľadať. Čaputovej mimovláda Via Iuris **dostávala od Sorosa** stovky tisíc eur… Ale hlavne, že z nás robia ruských agentov. **Sú na smiech.** Všetci vidia to **pokrytectvo slniečkarov** (25.5.2023).[193]*

---

[193] EL → THE LIBERAL MEDIA **SHAMELESSLY** SPREAD CONSPIRACY THEORIES: the Slovak corporate media **are sinking into such a quagmire that there is no bottom they haven't already broken through.** Even in North Korea they **don't play it this bluntly.** And television? What they **are perpetrating** is ultimate arrogance. They don't invite anyone from the opposition to RTVS – they **prattle on** with Šeliga and Gröhling. The two **losers** who were assisting Matovič and Sulík in the **devastation** of Slovakia for three years. Kovačič on Markíza TV **was bashing Robo Kaliňák like a madman.** Constant interruptions, butting into his speech, **the communication level of a pub on Fridays after midnight.** The media sphere has been taken over by **"sun-worshipping" extremist youth** with no education and no morals. America, liberalism, Russophobia and hatred for Smer – this is their mental horizon (29 May 2023) / THE ERA OF AMERICA IS ENDING – THAT'S WHY THEY FEAR US SO MUCH: Yesterday, the magazine *Zem a vek* celebrated its 10th anniversary. I was honoured to have the opportunity to speak and congratulate Tibor Rostas on his successful project. "Alternative" has succeeded in one thing. **They fear us.** Otherwise, they would not persecute us, otherwise they would not criminalize us. Recently, they have got a new censorship body – the Media Council. It has been **bullying** even the alternative media. Dírer and Závodský can **spread their "sun-worshipper" propaganda**, but *Zem a vek* and *Slobodný vysielač* must not give room to alternative views. **Double kilometre.** The Media Council is becoming a systemic **threat to freedom of speech.** Regime **thought police. The Gestapo.** After the election, order will have to be restored – censors have no place in a democracy. Čaputová's NGO Via Iuris **received hundreds of thousands of euros from Soros…** But they make Russian agents out of us. **They are ridiculous.** Everybody can see the **hypocrisy of the "sun worshippers"** (25 May 2023).

As can be seen, in the process of securitization in this case, not only verbs naming activities perceived by the majority society as distinctly negative (*bully, criminalize, bash, devastate, censor, threaten*) and politically deterrent (Gestapo, North Korea) and literary allusions (thought police, a reference to George Orwell's novel *1984*) are used at the lexical level. Expressive colloquial phrasemes such as *dávať na hulváta* (act shamelessly), *prepadať do stoky* (sink into quagmire), *prerážať dno* (no bottom they haven't already broken through), *ako zmyslov zbavený* (like a madman), *hrkútajú si* (prattle on), which reliably fulfil the linguistic purpose of approaching the potential voter, are also abundantly used. The rhetorical fervour gives rise to a certain linguistic creativity in the area of phraseology (the hyperbolizing *double kilometre* instead of the largely lexicalized, and thus in the role of a persuasive appeal no longer the expressive *double metre* [literal translation of a Slovak phrase carrying the meaning of *double standard*]), as well as the explication and substitution of the popular Slovak phrase *krčmová úroveň* (pub level), transformed into *the communication level of a pub on Fridays after midnight.* The target electorate of the SMER party will certainly be properly impressed by the phrases *hypocrisy of the sun worshippers, sun-worshipper propaganda*, as well as the unexpected allogical characterisation *sun-worshipper extremist youth without education and morals*, which in the context of the traditional semantics of the Slovak neologism *slniečkár* (free translation: *sun worshipper*) acts as an oxymoron (we had not encountered the term *uneducated sun worshipper* in Slovak political discourse before).

At the time when Blaha is trying his best to convince listeners of the "threat" to freedom of speech (in this case for leftist populists) in the public and mainstream media (which he describes as liberal), journalists and presenters from the aforementioned media are dealing with the issue of how to prevent the spread of disinformation and conspiracy theories. Their key question is posed as follows, "How to capture the diversity of events and ensure plurality of content while broadcasting in the public interest, being socially responsible and transparent?"[194] The answer to this question shows that we do not (as yet) have to fear any danger to "freedom of speech and media" in Slovakia today: "The most common critical narratives in the cases of controversial respondents coming into the mainstream media include: "legitimisation of a discredited respondent",

194   Bajaník, Ľ., & Frindt, M. (2022). Kríza „objektivizátorov" v televíznej žurnalistike. Spochybňovanie dôveryhodnosti respondentov v čase kríz. In A. Sámelová, M. Stanková, & J. Hacek (Eds.), *Fenomén 2022: Médiá a kríza autorít* (pp. 18–29). Bratislava: Univerzita Komenského v Bratislave.

"unacceptable opinion contrary to democratic principles", "deliberate spreading of disinformation", "subtle use of words and images to induce uncertainty in the subconscious of the audience", "pro-Russian, pro-Putin language", "normalising" (in the sense of disseminating propaganda), "the media give space to conspirational or, at least, alternative views, detached from reality".""[195]

Peace as an endangered entity. In the interpretation of left-wing populists, Ukraine itself, NATO and the US are responsible for the war in Ukraine. The Russian Federation ("our Slavic brothers") is innocent in this, and all that is needed to bring about immediate peace is for Ukrainians to give up their original territories occupied by the Russian Federation (hereinafter, the RF). The idea that the RF would withdraw its troops and return the occupied territory has not appeared even once in the discourse of SMER politicians since the invasion of Ukraine on 24 February 2022. They keep repeating the Kremlin narrative "the RF was forced into armed conflict by NATO and Ukrainian nationalists" and successfully incite Slovak citizens to "marches for peace" and other forms of expressing disagreement with the aid of the Slovak Republic to the invaded state (Ukraine). Day after day they tell their audience that the threat to peace is "the Americans and the Zelensky regime", and then marvel at the truly remarkable results of their own securitization:

SL → *Slovensko ma neprestáva prekvapovať a cítim neuveriteľnú hrdosť. Podľa prieskumu* **amerických pätolízalov z Globsecu** *rapídne klesla dôveryhodnosť NATO na Slovensku a väčšina Slovákov viní za vojnu na Ukrajine Američanov či* **Zelenského režim.** *Napriek tomu, že liberálne médiá od rána do večera* **hrajú americkú propagandu,** *ľudí na Slovensku* **neoblbli.** *Filozof Kant kedysi definoval osvietenstvo ako* **odvahu používať vlastný rozum.** *A Slováci to napriek* **veľkonážnej protiruskej propagande** *dokážu. Držíme sa hodnoty mieru. A patríme k tým* **najkritickejším národom** *v Európe, čo sa týka USA a ich* **vojnovej propagandy.** *Nie, my Slováci* **nebudeme súčasťou mašinérie,** *ktorá chce len zabíjať, otročiť a vykorisťovať. Chceme mier, slobodu a* **slovanskú vzájomnosť.** *Ďakujem, že som Slovák* (26.5.2023)[196]

---

195 Bajaník, & Frindt, 2022, p. 23

196 EL → Slovakia never ceases to amaze me, and I feel incredible pride. According to a poll by **the American minions from Globsec,** NATO's credibility in Slovakia has plummeted and the majority of Slovaks blame the Americans or **the Zelensky regime** for the war in Ukraine. Despite the fact that the liberal media **are playing American propaganda** around the clock, the people of Slovakia **have not been fooled.** The philosopher Kant once defined the Enlightenment as **the courage to use one's own reason.** And the Slovaks can do it, despite **the heavy-weight anti-Russian propaganda.** We stick to the value of peace. And we are one of **the most critical nations** in Europe when it comes to the USA and its **war propaganda.** No, we Slovaks **will not be part of a machine** that only wants to kill, enslave and exploit. We want peace, freedom and **Slavic reciprocity.** I am thankful to be a Slovak (26 May 2023)

On the side of evil (threat) as we can see *the Zelensky regime* (not *the government*, always *the regime*, a word with extremely negative semantics), *the American minions from Globsec* (it is not clear why the Slovak pejorative expression *pätolízač* is replaced by the equally pejorative bohemism *pätolízal* in the Slovak original), *American propaganda, heavy-weight anti-Russian propaganda* (distinctive hyperbolization) and *war propaganda, a machine that only wants to kill, enslave, and exploit* (negative semantic gradation). More than enough intimidating expressions for one paragraph, in contrast to which Blaha uses the imaginary, abstract idea, glorified by Slovaks for two centuries, of Slavic reciprocity (for which he does not even need to look for historical references and logical arguments, it is an inherent and bulletproof narrative of all Slovak populist demagogues). And finally, (not only in Blaha) the idea of Slavic reciprocity and Pan-Slavism always results in uncritical Russophilia. The author flatters the audience who have the courage to use their own reason ("elevates" them to the level of philosophers and compares them to Kant himself) and pathetically thanks (God? fate? parents?) for being Slovak (the most critical nation in Europe). The discursive strategy of "you and I are true patriots, the others are traitors", however, quite often (as in this case) it takes on the vector of civic nationalism and superiority over other nations. And this is the foundation for the following idea which fully corresponds to the Kremlin's plans, although it is not explicitly mentioned here, and will only be implemented if SMER wins the 2023 parliamentary elections:

SL → *POĎME VYTVORIŤ STREDOEURÓPSKY OSTROV MIERU: kvôli Západu vo vojne* **zbytočne umierajú** *Ukrajinci. Američania sa boja, že v strednej Európe sa vytvorí silný blok mierových krajín – orbánovské Maďarsko, neutrálne Rakúsko a po septembri Slovensko na čele s Robertom Ficom. Takýto* **ostrov mieru** *by mohol postupne oslabovať ich zástupnú vojnu proti Rusku, na ktorej* **kráľovsky zarábajú americké zbrojovky** *aj energetické spoločnosti. Aj preto tu* **americkí poskokovia kmitajú ako včeličky.** *Čaputová na post premiéra dosadila* **Sorosovho človeka,** *vojnové* **mimovládky** *organizujú* **militaristický sabat,** *na ktorom sa budú pretekať, kto viac nenávidí Rusko a kto pošle Ukrajine viac zbraní. Takto to vyhovuje Bidenovej administratíve a* **jej hlavnému sponzorovi Sorosovi.** *Veď ako výstižne skonštatoval americký podnikateľ Elon Musk,* "**Soros nenávidí ľudstvo**". **Americký liberálny establišment** *medzitým* **prekračuje všetky červené čiary** *a ženie svet do jadrovej vojny. Už stačilo zabíjania. Prestaňme posielať zbrane na Ukrajinu, prestaňme s nenávisťou a prebuďme diplomatov. Poďme vytvoriť* **stredoeurópsky ostrov mieru** – *už v septembri* (24.05.2023).[197]

---

197   EL → LET'S CREATE A MID-EUROPEAN ISLAND OF PEACE: Ukrainians **are dying pointlessly** in war because of the West. Americans fear that a strong bloc of peace-loving countries will be formed in Central Europe – Orbán's Hungary,

In one paragraph, the ideal *island of peace*, is mentioned; its creation can be achieved by merely giving your vote in the elections to the "Central European peacemakers" and there will be an end to the killing, an end to the threat of nuclear war (which probably worries Slovaks more than the *pointlessly dying Ukrainians*). In the context of the analysed paragraph, the call *to stop the hate* sounds almost comically absurd, since it is precisely the evocation of fear and the associated hatred that is the focus of most of its content and the lexical devices: the updated phrasemes *cross all the red lines, buzzing around like little bees*. Who *buzzes like a bee*? Of course, the main "threat" to peace, namely *the American stooges*, which, in Blaha's speech acts, represent a derogatory and derisive label for NGOs. Immediately, their allegedly Jewish background is alluded to: *the war NGOs organize a militaristic sabbath* (a Latinized form of the Jewish Sabbath), which is one of the popular conspiracy theories on the Slovak disinformation scene, references to which can be immediately decoded by potential voters of SMER. And the mythicised name of Soros, who *hates humanity*, appears in the manipulative tactics again and again (while also using the discourse strategy of appealing to authority, which in this case is the world-famous American businessman Elon Musk). Soros's name appearing three times in three consecutive sentences seems redundant to the point of being intrusive, but it is typical of and proven by Blaha's discourse in terms of securitisation; for after all, thanks to his securitisation tactics, he is able to state with pleasure the following (and for a democratic EU state extremely disturbing) fact:

SL → *86% SLOVÁKOV ODMIETA POSIELANIE ZBRANÍ NA UKRAJINU - **RIADNA FACKA** PRE NAĎA A ČAPUTOVÚ. V Denníku N si urobili prieskum, z ktorého **vyskakujú z okna**. Neviem sa prestať smiať. Vyšlo im, že iba 14% Slovákov chce posielať zbrane na Ukrajinu. Čiže - 86% to nechce! Podľa prieskumu Denníka N zároveň vyšlo,*

---

neutral Austria and, after September, Slovakia, led by Robert Fico. Such **an island of peace** could gradually weaken their proxy war against Russia, on which both **the US armaments** and energy **companies are making royal profits**. That's also why **the American stooges are buzzing around like little bees**. Čaputová has put **a Soros man** in the post of Prime Minister, **the war NGOs** are organizing **a militaristic sabbath** where they **will compete to see who hates Russia more** and who will send more weapons to Ukraine. This is what suits the Biden administration and **its main sponsor, Soros**. After all, as the American businessman Elon Musk succinctly put it, **"Soros hates humanity"**. Meanwhile, **the American liberal establishment is crossing all red lines and driving the world into nuclear war.** There has been enough killing. Let's stop sending weapons to Ukraine, let's stop the hate and let's wake up diplomats. Let's create **a Central-European island of peace** – in September (24 May 2023).

že až 42% ľudí považuje USA za hrozbu. A iba 14% za spojenca. **Kdepak soudruzi z**
juesej udělali chybu? *Predpokladám, že tých 14% milovníkov amerických vojen bude*
tých istých 14%, čo chce posielať zbrane na Ukrajinu a viesť **americký džihád** *proti Rusku*
(26.04.2023).[198]

The ironizing tone indicates absolute contentment with the results of their daily
efforts in the field of information warfare, and the sense of victory is underscored
by the lexical devices used: colloquial phrasemes *riadna facka* (*proper slap in the*
face), *vyskakujú z okna* (*jumping out the window*), as well as a satirical adaptation
(substitution) of one of the most popular precedent expressions in Slovakia
from the iconic Czech film Pelíšky (1999) *Kdepak asi udělali soudruzi z NDR*
chybu? (translation of the original *Where did the comrades from the GDR make*
a mistake? compared to the adjusted *Where did the comrades from youesey make*
a mistake?). The use of the political metaphor of *jihad* (in the analysed case, *the*
American jihad against Russia) is popular among Slovak actors of securitizing
discourse (also in the instance of propagators of Kremlin disinformation
narratives), which leads to a deliberate simplification of an otherwise complex
religious concept, and "the fact that jihad is almost exclusively invoked in the
mass media in association with terrorism, radicalism, and religious extremism
… leads to the demonization of Islam as such…. and to the reinforcement of
uncritical Islamophobia along with the rejection of anything alien, different,
outside the framework of established patterns of behaviour and which, after all,
media producers and recipients are not at all interested in critically examining."[199]
This form of "hate speech" metaphorization that demonizes phenomena and
concepts of another culture, leads to the emptying of their original meanings
and to a solely negative, one-sided perception by Slovaks, who due to similar
efforts to stigmatize other nations and religions, also belong (according to Blaha's
phrase) "among the most critical nations in Europe".

---

198   EL → 86 % OF SLOVAKS REJECT SENDING WEAPONS TO UKRAINE – **A**
       PROPER SLAP IN THE FACE FOR NAĎ AND ČAPUTOVÁ. In Denník N they
       conducted a poll which **makes them jump out the window**. I can't stop laughing.
       They found out that only 14 % of Slovaks want to send arms to Ukraine. That is –
       86 % don't want it! At the same time, according to the Denník N poll, 42 % of people
       consider the US a threat. And only 14 % as an ally. **Where did the comrades from**
       the "youesey" go wrong? I suppose that the 14 % who love American wars will be
       the same 14 % who want to send weapons to Ukraine and wage an **American jihad**
       against Russia. (26 April 2023)
199   Skačan, J. (2017). Critical analysis of media discourse: Islam, Jihad and Islamophobia.
       Philosophica Critica, 3(2), 15–33.

As illustrated by the example of the thematization of the narrative "we are for peace" and "Russia was forced to take this step", the statements of Ľuboš Blaha, the Deputy Chairman of the Smer-SD Ľ. addressing Russia are characterized by "complete identification with the official stance of Kremlin on the one hand, and on the other by ignoring verified facts and spreading disinformation, distorting contexts and sharp attacks on the political and opinion opponents of the current Russian regime. The ironic style of Blaha's argumentation often creates an infantile impression. The timing, diction and content of the posts show that their author is adapting to the main trend of Russian state propaganda."[200] Indeed, it is more than timely; Putin's European fifth column (of which Blaha is the most prominent representative in Slovakia) and its agitations against Ukraine and EU policy are of paramount importance in the current critical phase of the war. One must agree with the political scientist's observation that "the ironic style of Blaha's argumentation often strikes an infantile impression". The politician, who positions himself as a champion of peace now that Russia has unleashed a war, did not hesitate to childishly boast about Russia's new Avangard ballistic missile back in 2019 and did not even wonder what such weapons could possibly be used for. Mesežnikov and Bartoš quote from Blaha's posts at the time:

SL → „*Rusko vynašlo novú jadrovú superzbraň. Systémy USA by novú raketu Avangard nedokázali ani zameraľ, tobôž zostreliľ. Šach, mat. Rusi dali Američanom šach-mat … to je to zaostalé Rusko, z ktorého sa vysmievajú na Západe. Zdá sa, že sa dosmiali. Ehm, kdepak soudruzi z juesej udelali chybu? Západným mocnostiam akosi nejde karta.*"[201]

As we have already observed in the first part of the chapter, from the lexical viewpoint, Blaha is extremely redundant; he invariably adjusts the winged phrase from the film Pelíšky in the same form (*where did the comrades from the youesey go wrong*), and doesn't hesitate to use the same colloquial expressions in the same paragraph to emphasize the idea and escalate the emotion (*Checkmate. Russians have given Americans checkmate*).

---

200 Mesežnikov G., & Bartoš J. (2021). *Kto hrá ruskú ruletu na Slovensku.* Bratislava: Inštitút pre verejné otázky, p. 98.

201 EL → "Russia has invented a new nuclear superweapon. The US systems could not even target, let alone shoot down, the new Avangard missile. Checkmate. Russians have given Americans checkmate … this is the underdeveloped Russia that the West makes fun of. Their laughing seems to have come to an end. Um, where did the comrades from the youesey go wrong? Somehow the Western powers haven't got the right cards to play." (Mesežnikov & Bartoš, 2021: 92).

From Blaha's statuses articulating the "threat to peace" it is obvious that if the Avangard missiles admired and praised by him were flying straight to Slovakia, our skilful securitisation actor would be able to explain to Slovaks that only NATO, Soros and the Bandera followers are to blame. "In justifying Russia's actions Blaha uses the method of ideologically and politically motivated selection. It rests on his conviction that the current Russian regime is always right and will always prevail over the West. This is quite reminiscent of the matrix of Soviet and communist propaganda from 1917 to 1991 (propaganda of success, an attack against the decadent bourgeois West, condemnation of the regime's critics, support for the repression of opponents, concealment of setbacks and failures). By this setting, the deputy chairman of Smer-SD completely aligns himself with the protagonists of the current Russian state media-propaganda machine, advocating the Kremlin's superpower policy."[202]

The threat to the lives of Slovaks has been one of the successful vectors of securitization since the start of the war in Ukraine in February 2022, in the sense of the potential mobilization of Slovak males over the age of 18. This was an immensely powerful narrative of the Slovak disinformation scene, despite the fact that it did not in any way correlate with reality (we have a professional army, we are a member of NATO, etc.). In this case, *facts are nothing, playing on emotion and fear are everything*, and that is why a Slovak journalist remarks: *Get ready*, **you will have to recruit for the war** *against Russia. If NATO sends troops to Ukraine,* **Slovaks will** *be the first to* **go to die.** *Such warnings have flooded social networks in recent weeks too, along with appeals to refuse emergency military service. That too is the reason why the number of such applications has increased almost 30-fold compared to last year. According to Martina Kakaščíková, the Defence Ministry spokesperson, as confirmed to Pravda, "More than 40 thousand citizens have applied for placement in alternative service". As she indicated, the Defence Ministry attributes this enormous increase to Russian hybrid operations with the help of the opposition parties Smer and Republika: "In any case, given the campaign from Russia through the Slovak opposition, we are not surprised by this figure."*[203]

202   Mesežnikov G., & Bartoš J. (2021). *Kto hrá ruskú ruletu na Slovensku.* Bratislava: Inštitút pre verejné otázkym, p. 89.

203   Hutko, D. (2023, February 14). Klamstvá, strašenie aj reálne obavy. Slováci vo veľkom odopierajú vojenskú službu. *Pravda.* https://spravy.pravda.sk/domace/clanok/657 055-vyhlasenie-o-odopreti-vykonu-mimoriadnej-sluzby-podalo-vyse-40-tisic-obcanov/

Human life is an extraordinarily "gratifying" object of reference. Inducing fear for "dear life"[204] is a very easy pre-election populist strategy of parties struggling for power. Blaha, of course, did his best to present this "threat" to Slovaks frightened by the war in the neighbouring state in a most realistic and repulsive fashion:

SL → *Ľudia sa oprávnene boja – vo vláde sú dnes* **extrémni vojnoví štváči,** *ktorí dokonca chcú ako prvá krajina na svete oficiálne poslať stíhačky na Ukrajinu, čo môže mať nedozerné následky. Slovensko môžu svojou hlúposťou* **uvrhnúť** *do strašnej vojny. A v takýchto situáciách by bola* **mobilizácia** *úplne logickým* **vyústením ich tuposti a nezodpovednosti.** *NAKA vraj spúšťa trestné konanie ohľadom našich výrokov, že na Slovensku hrozí mobilizácia. Včera sa tým vyhrážal Naď na TA3 a už dnes* **Hamran** *zmobilizoval svojich* **gestapáčikov** *– gratulujeme. A základom celého vášho poznania povinne musia* **byť propagandistické vyhlásenia notorického klamára** *Naďa (vtedajší minister obrany SR, poznámka autorov) o tom, že mobilizáciu neplánuje – úplne ma upokojil, veď keď nás naposledy takto Slovákov ubezpečil, že nepošle S-300 na Ukrajinu, poslal ju tam do niekoľkých dní* (20.2.2023).[205]

Although the assertions are not based on facts, the emotionally impressive statements about *extreme warmongers* dreaming of *plunging Slovakia into a terrible war* could not go unanswered (mostly by the population incapable of critical thinking), and this can be considered as an exceedingly successful securitization, which is confirmed by information from the Slovak media: "A record has been broken: more than 40 thousand men refused to fight for Slovakia. Naď also blames

---

204 Fear for one's dear life, fight for one's dear life, their life is at stake are popular and aptly Slovak phrases, emphasizing the urgency of the threat; literal translations of the Slovak version are "bare life" or "naked life".

205 EL → People are justifiably afraid – there are **extreme warmongers** in the government today who even want to be the first country in the world to officially send fighter jets to Ukraine, which could have unprecedented consequences. With their stupidity, they can **plunge Slovakia into a terrible war.** And in such situations, mobilization would be **a perfectly logical outcome of their bluntness and irresponsibility.** NAKA (the National Criminal Agency, authors' note) is said to be launching criminal proceedings regarding our statements that there is a threat of mobilization in Slovakia. Yesterday, Naď (then Minister of Defence of the Slovak Republic, authors' note) threatened to do so on TA3 and today **Hamran** (the President of the Slovak Police, authors' note) has already **mobilized his little gestapo** – congratulations. And the foundation of all your knowledge **must be the propagandist statements of the notorious liar** Naď that he was not planning to mobilize – he completely reassured me, because the last time he assured us Slovaks that he was not going to send the S-300 to Ukraine, he sent it there within a few days (20.2.2023).

Fico and Blaha. Naďblames Smer politicians, led by the chairman Robert Fico, for reducing the state's defence capacity. It is precisely because of people like Fico and Blaha that the country's defences are being undermined. Over 40 thousand people have submitted such a form, which, by the way, is completely unnecessary. Some politicians have poured oil on the flame too. For example, Milan Uhrík, the head of the Republic party, wrote on Facebook about the 'invitation to war'. Later, Smer also took up the topic. The party's deputy chairman, Ľuboš Blaha, said that Slovaks were in real danger of going to fight in Ukraine. 'Families will lose their sons, women will lose their husbands', he claimed at a press conference."[206]

Human and civic dignity, as mentioned in Chapter I, is one of the fundamental reference objects in which the securitizing actor creates a sense of threat to social acceptance, dignity, education, recognition, and respect. Blaha does it in a straightforward manner, which could hardly be called sophisticated, presenting as an unquestionable fact, alleged insults to his potential voters made by liberals, government officials, NGOs, and yet he never refers to specific statements of this kind:

> SL → *liberáli ľuďmi až tak veľmi **pohŕdajú**, že väčšinu národa **označia za dezolátov** (1 June 2023) / **Prezidentka** dnes vyslala odkaz státisícom voličom Smeru, že nás nenávidí, **opovrhuje nami** a že pre ňu nie sme občanmi Slovenskej republiky (10 May 2023)/ To fakt za toto štrngali ľudia v 89-om? Ak nemáš názor ako Čaputová, Tódová, Káčer či Valášek, tak **si dezolát**. A treba ti zobrať slobodu slova. (19 April 2023)/ Izolovaná bublinka okolo Čaputovej, PS a Hegera, ktorá je v ťažkej menšine, ale majú v rukách médiá a mimovládky po 86% národa **vyvreskujú**, že **všetci sme dezoláti**, extrémisti a ruskí agenti. To čo má byť? (26 April 2023).[207]*

---

206   Kyseľ, T. (2023, Febraury 13). Padol rekord: viac ako 40-tisíc mužov odmietlo bojovať za Slovensko. *Aktuality.sk.* https://www.aktuality.sk/clanok/dXLDt83/padol-rek ord-viac-ako-40-tisic-muzov-odmietlo-bojovat-za-slovensko-nad-vini-aj-fica-s- blahom/

207   EL → **liberals despise** people so much that they **label** the majority of the nation **as the trash** (1 June 2023) / **The President** today delivered a message to hundreds of thousands of Smer voters that she **detested us,** despised us and that for her we are not citizens of the Slovak Republic (10 May 2023)/ Is this really what the people were struggling for in '89? If you do not share the opinion of Čaputová, Tódová, Káčer or Valášek**, you are trash, a misfit. And you should be denied your freedom of speech. (19 April 2023)/** The isolated little bubble around Čaputová, Progresívne Slovensko party and Heger, is in a striking minority, but they have the media in their hands, and NGOs **yell** at 86 % of the nation **that we are all trash,** extremists and Russian agents. What's that supposed to be? (26 April 2023).

The people, whose interests are supposedly defended only by the SMER party, are labelled by liberals *as trash* (where? when? by whom specifically? we do not find this in Blaha's posts). The nation *is despised* even by the President herself; *you are trash* if you are not of the right opinion, *NGOs yell that WE ALL ARE trash.* Securitisation actor Blaha "selflessly identifies himself" with a nation whose human dignity is threatened, and the discourse strategy *I am with you, we are one group* is expressed by the idea *we are all trash*, and it is an extremely effective strategy. This case reflects the notion that 'identifying with a group that defines itself against the mainstream can be a source of pride, despite the threat of social stigmatization, but in particular it allows members to stand out in the crowd and highlight their separateness. The more distinct such a group is externally, the more conformist it is internally. Thus (paradoxically) conformity becomes a powerful expression of difference. The perceptual enhancement of one's own group's distinctiveness happens by pointing out intergroup differences and highlighting intragroup similarities."[208] It is particularly the creation of a sense of intra-group unity, when everyone is "in the same boat" and everyone is equally and unfairly humiliated by labels such as "trash, misfits", that is supposed to create a sense of hatred for people from another group and to give as many addressees as possible a sense of unity with the party that defends their human dignity and rejects humiliation from the existing government (which in real life has never happened).

The threat to public and individual health is also a reliable strategy for inducing fear, because what do we fear for more than our own health? And this opens up a broad range of opportunities for emotional blackmail and linguistic manipulation:

SL → *CHCÚ NÁS UKRAJINCI OTRÁVIŤ?!* **Brusel** už vyše polroka **necháva zamorovať** Slovensko a celú strednú Európu **nebezpečnou ukrajinskou pšenicou** a Hegerova vláda nič. Toto je doslova **zločin proti ľudskosti**. **Trasorítky** v slovenskej vláde a Prezidentskom paláci **majú svojich občanov na saláme.** **Skáču tak, ako arogantný Brusel píska.** Toto je **učebnicové ohrozenie národnej bezpečnosti.** Ale ako vždy, vláde **sú ukradnuté** záujmy Slovákov a tak ukrajinským podvodníkom **dovolila ohroziť zdravie našich občanov** – ak toto nie je **vlastizrada**, tak čo potom? A je mi srdečne jedno, čo si o tom myslia **bruselskí technokráti**, ktorí vyše polroka nechali strednú Európu **žrať chemické kokteily z Ukrajiny.** Im je zjavne **jedno, že pokapeme.** Tu sa krásne ukazuje, že Slovensko si musí chrániť svoju národnú suverenitu a **nesmieme byť len poslušnou kolóniou Bruselu a Washingtonu,**

---

208 Hatoková, M. (2014). Sme pri rozhodovaní obeťami sociálnych vplyvov? In E. Ballová Mikušková, & V. Čavojová (Eds.), *Rozhodovanie v kontexte kognície, osobnosti a emócií. Súčasné trendy v rozhodovaní* (pp. 151–156). Bratislava: SAV.

ako chcú liberáli. Už stačilo! Slovensko potrebuje vládu, ktorá bude chrániť Slovákov – tu *už **ide naozaj o zdravie a o život!** Už včera bolo neskoro!* (17 April 2023)[209]

Securitisation, in this case assumes, hypertrophied proportions, because it compares the incomparable, namely *dangerous Ukrainian wheat* (which a propos is also used by Ukrainians themselves and the essence of its harmfulness lies only in the fact that, that it does not yet comply with all of the strict EU food standards) with *a crime against humanity* which most of the Slovak population associates with mass murder, genocide, torture, deportation, enslavement or other atrocities committed against the civilian population. All the more fear the listed associations must evoke in the addressee, whose cowardly government (the colloquial metaphor of *trasorítky = sissies*) *does not give a damn* (literal translation of the colloquial Slovak phraseme is *has it on salami*), because it *eats out of Brussels' hand* (literal translation of the Slovak colloquial phraseme is *jump as Brussels whistles*). Traditionally strong concepts such as *treason* and *threat to national security* (which, moreover, is *textbook* quality, i.e., unquestionable) alternate with vulgarisms **to guzzle** *chemical cocktails from Ukraine* from which we all will **drop dead**. But all it takes is to vote for the right party (*that will protect Slovaks*) and we will no longer be *an obedient colony of Brussels and Washington* and *the health and life* of Slovaks will be saved. Clear ideas in an impressive linguistic package. Another of the urgent threats that can only be eliminated by participating in the elections and voting for SMER.

Threats to family and traditional Slovak values in Blaha's discourse are articulated less frequently, but the established vector is clear and fully corresponds to the popular narratives of contemporary Kremlin propaganda:

209　EL → DO UKRAINIANS WANT TO POISON US?! **Brussels lets** Slovakia and all of Central Europe **be contaminated with dangerous Ukrainian wheat** for more than half a year, and the Heger government does nothing. This is literally **a crime against humanity**. The **sissies** in the Slovak Government and the Presidential Palace **don't give a damn about their citizens. They eat out of arrogant Brussels hand**. This is **a textbook threat to national security**. But as usual, the government **doesn't care** about the interests of Slovaks, so it has **allowed Ukrainian crooks to endanger the health of our citizens** – if this isn't **treason**, then what is? And I don't care what **the Brussels technocrats**, who have let Central Europe **guzzle chemical cocktails from Ukraine** for more than half a year, think about this. They obviously **don't care that we will drop dead**. This beautifully shows that Slovakia must protect its national sovereignty and **we must not** just **be an obedient colony of Brussels and Washington**, as liberals want us to be. That's enough! Slovakia needs a government that will protect Slovaks – this is really **a question of health and life!** Yesterday was already too late! (17 April 2023)

SL → *využime čas, kým Progresívci nevyhlásia rodinu za prekonanú inštitúciu a kým* **mamičky, oteckov a detičky nenahradia osobami jedna, dva, tri, štyri.** *Títo dúhoví* **popletenci** *nikdy nepochopia, čo je to láska k rodine, láska k vlasti, láska k Slovensku (27 May 2023) ZACHRÁŇME NAŠE DETI PRED VYMÝVANÍM MOZGOV: Na besede v Žiline sa ľudia pýtali, ako je možné, že sa už dnes aj na základných školách pretláča liberálna ideológia. "Prepisujú dejiny a šíria nenávisť voči Rusku," upozorňoval nahnevaný pán. "Toto musíme zastaviť!" (24 April 2023). My nie sme* **ružová ľavica,** *my* **neriešime sexuálne menšiny.** *My sme červená ľavica a riešime pracujúcich Slovákov* (18 April 2023)[210]

The touching diminutives of *moms, dads and babies* stand out impressively as opposed to the "cold" *persons one, two, three, four,* a favourite narrative of Vladimir Putin, which he repeats endlessly in every thematically appropriate (but also thematically irrelevant) speech. "In a number of interactions, Vladimir Putin's statements on the topic of gender equality and same-sex rights in Western countries resonate. He criticizes the West for introducing terms such as "parent number 1" and "parent number 2", which he says is "on the verge of a crime against humanity". The aim of these disinformation narratives is to give the public the false impression that Western society, especially its value-setting associated with tolerance and multiculturalism, will lead to moral depravity and deviance. On the contrary, Russia is portrayed as a guarantor and defender of "traditional values.""[211] Derogatory and even degrading to the LGBT community are the pejorative labels of **rainbow deluded fools** and **the pink left,** but the notion of political correctness is merely a liberal invention for left-wing populists and Blaha downplays it in his Telegram as *"glorious liberal political correctness, which is just their rainbow masquerade"* (26 March 2023).

As we can observe, the securitization vectors in Blaha's discourse in 2023 compared to 2021 were directed at differently presented referential objects

---

210   EL → *let's use the time until Progressives declare the family an obsolete institution and until* **moms, dads, and babies are replaced by persons one, two, three, four.** *These* **rainbow-deluded fools** *will never understand what love for family, love for country, love for Slovakia is (27 May 2023) LET'S SAVE OUR CHILDREN FROM BRAINWASHING: At a discussion in Žilina, people asked how it was possible that liberal ideology was already being pushed in elementary schools. "They are rewriting history and spreading hatred against Russia", an angry man pointed out. "We must stop this!" (24 April 2023). We are not* **the pink left;** *we* **do not deal with sexual minorities.** *We are the red left, and we deal with working Slovaks (18 April 2023)*

211   Takács, D. (2021, November 8). Slovenské dezinformačné weby ako piliere proruských naratívov na Slovensku. *Infosecurity.sk.* https://infosecurity.sk/dezinfo/slovenske-dezinformacne-weby-ako-piliere-proruskych-narativov-na-slovensku/

(democracy, family and traditional Slovak values, public and individual health, the lives of Slovaks as well as their human and civil dignity, peace, media freedom and freedom of speech); nevertheless, the speech tactics aimed at creating a sense of threat in potential voters remained unchanged. Through the metaphorization of a conflictogenic nature, Blaha, the experienced securitization actor, ironizes, condemns, stigmatizes. He resemanticizes established ideologemes, adapts colloquial phrasemes and precedent expressions, consistently employs the same intimidating precedent names, uses emotionally-coloured expressions, stylistically symptomatic lexis, hyperboles and substandard lexis (sociolects, jargonisms and vulgarisms) with an explicitly persuasive and implicitly manipulative intent. Considering the mere fact that the opposition managed to push through pre-term parliamentary elections in September 2023, as well as the pre-election statistics (extremely favourable for SMER), and especially the alarming results of the Globsec comparative poll in May 2023 (which shows, that up to 51 % of Slovaks think that the responsibility for the war in Ukraine lies with "the West, which provoked Russia" and with Ukraine itself), we must conclude that the securitisation efforts of the SMER Deputy Chairman have not been wasted.

Very convincing in this regard are the reflections of Martin Gladiš, an expert on contemporary Slovak media discourse, in terms of the currently broadly discussed crisis of communication in the online environment and, consequently, in the media and public space.

"We are witnessing social elites being reluctant to participate in public communication, and the 'vacant' place in the media space is being occupied mainly by those segments of society that do not have the potential for its qualitative improvement; on the contrary, they bring into the public (media) discourse a moral baseness that is symptomatic of the de-classed and marginalized segments of society, which – understandably – leads to the subsequent vulgarization of the entire public space. This modus operandi is being adopted – whether on the grounds of natural predisposition or for purely pragmatic (utilitarian, self-interested) reasons – by the top representatives of political parties and movements, as can be observed on the domestic political scene… However, this is in sharp contrast to the role and position of a (political or social) leader who communicates factually, sophisticatedly, without violation of communication rules, without insulting, humiliating or ridiculing opponents, and through his or her communication deliberately and systematically refines the public space. Instead, however, we can observe how the content (lexis, vocabulary) and form (mode of delivery, manner) of public discourse are becoming increasingly coarse, especially under the influence of communication in the online space, which also seems to be acquiring the symptoms of a "standard" in the media and public space. We believe that this state of affairs can be described as a crisis of communication, and one of its consequences is the (not only verbal) aggression that has been transferred from the online environment to real life."[212]

A more concise characterization of the essence of Blaha's securitization efforts (both at the level of discourse strategies and speech tactics) and their social consequences would be hard to find. In conclusion, we would like to point out that in this context the acute question of his responsibility for his choice of linguistic means and meanings of speech acts arises, since conflictogenic metaphors and the lower standard lexis inevitably steer the discourse towards an increase in aggression. However, to date, the question remains unanswered. Tensions are rising in society, and this suits political actors very well, because in order to increase the number of adherents, securitization is the shortest and surest route, since presenting dangers to a certain community immediately binds it together and becomes the most convenient form of ideological consolidation.

212 Gladiš, M. (2022). Kríza autorít ako kríza komunikácie. In A. Sámelová, M. Stanková, & J. Hacek (Eds.), *Fenomén 2022: Médiá a kríza autorít* (pp. 9–18). Bratislava: Univerzita Komenského v Bratislave.

IV. Conflictogenic metaphors in Robert Fico's securitization discourse

Contemporary experts in the field of metaphorology have arrived at the conclusion that in parallel with the deepening of the social crisis (political, economic, national) in the speeches of politicians, the quantity of so-called conflictogenic metaphors is clearly increasing, which indicates their efforts to enhance the manipulative effect of their own speech acts and to deepen social tension. This chapter will focus on the speech acts of Robert Fico[213] (the chairman of the – at the moment – opposition party SMER – SD) in order to analyse how conflictogenic metaphors facilitate the process of effective securitization. The material for exemplification is extracted from Fico's official Facebook page: https://www.facebook.com/robertficosk (194,000 followers) from 1 January 2022 to 27 September 2022. We point out how the process of metaphorization creates a sense of threat to the referent objects.

In the statements of the societally influential securitization actor Robert Fico[214] the democratic values of Slovak society, the values of the rule of law and the social state, the standard of living of Slovaks and even the independence, sovereignty and statehood of Slovakia are presented as referent objects (threatened entities):

---

213 Some of these examples have already been analysed in the article by Dulebová I. (2022). Conflictogenic Metaphors in R. Fico's Securitisation Discourse. In. R. Štefančík (Ed.), *Jazyk a politika: na pomedzí lingvistiky a politológie VII.* (pp. 76–87). Bratislava: Ekonóm.

214 Social influence is assessed, among other things, by its influence on social networks, and in this respect Fico has no equal on the Slovak political scene; this is particularly important in terms of our research, since the success of a securitization move depends heavily on the social authority of the securitizing actor. Fico is continuously progressing in his successful presence on social networks, which was also noted by Filip Struhárik in his paper *Fico wins on Facebook…*: "In the first quarter of 2023, Fico had ten videos on his Facebook page that had more than 200 thousand views. Many others surpassed the hundred-thousand mark. The good choice of content that is effective on the social network has also made Fico the most successful politician on Facebook. In three months, his posts had nearly 1.3 million interactions, i.e., likes, comments and shares". Struhárik, F. (2023, July 4). Fico vyhráva na Facebooku, Smeru sa darí aj na TikToku. Instagram je úplne iný svet. *Denník N.* https://denn ikn.sk/3456131/fico-vyhrava-na-facebooku-smeru-sa-dari-aj-na-tiktoku-instag ram-je-uplne-iny-svet

SL → *hodnoty právneho a sociálneho štátu sa **otriasajú v základoch*** / *Táto vláda **zdevastovala** Slovensko právne, sociálne a aj ekonomicky* / *Obrovský pokles životnej úrovne Slovákov je **tragickou vizitkou** neschopnosti terajšej vlády a jediným východiskom sú predčasné voľby* / *Putin môže nechať túto zimu Európu **vymrznúť*** / *Slovensko v rukách tejto vlády **míľovými krokmi stráca vlastnú zvrchovanosť**, suverenitu a aj štátnosť!* / *politici ako Heger a Čaputová vojdú do učebníc dejepisu ako **najväčší likvidátori slovenskej suverenity*** / *Prezidentka len **plní pokyny americkej ambasády**.*[215]

In the case of securitization, the aforementioned topics are defined as existentially threatened, which should serve as a "compelling reason" to take measures that go well beyond the boundaries of established political governance. One of the main outcomes of securitization (clearly indicating its success) was the referendum leading to early elections: *a group of political parties has decided to organize a petition campaign asking the President of the Slovak Republic to announce a referendum on the fall of the current government of the Slovak Republic and on changes to the Constitution of the Slovak Republic… we will do everything possible to ensure that a referendum on pre-term elections can be held in the autumn on the day of the municipal and regional elections* (status of Robert Fico on 15 June 2022).

The objective of the following analysis is to examine how Fico justifies the necessity of an immediate referendum and a change of government through strong metaphorization, and how his pejorative "linguistic arguments" contribute to the long-term trend of securitization of Slovakia's political and economic independence (as the main "threatened" referent object), which, together with Smer-SD, is insistently raised by the other opposition parties as well.

The nature of our analysis is not that of political science (it does not evaluate the content relevance of the statements nor does it examine which statements are disinformation, deliberate lies, disingenuous distortion of facts, conspiracy theories); the subject of the analysis is the linguistic (mainly lexical) level of the politician's statements, on the basis of which we intend to demonstrate how

---

215   EL → the values of the rule of law and the social state are being **shaken to their foundations** / This government has **devastated** Slovakia in legal, social and economic terms / The huge decline in the standard of living of Slovaks is **a tragic sign** of the incompetence of the current government and the only way out is pre-term elections / Putin may let Europe **freeze to death** this winter / Slovakia is **losing its independence**, sovereignty and statehood at the hands of this government **by leaps and bounds!** / Politicians like Heger and Čaputová will go down in the history books as **the biggest destroyers of Slovak sovereignty** / the President is just **following the instructions of the American embassy.**

metaphorization increases the persuasive, manipulative effect of speech acts and thus helps the process of securitization.

4.1 Conflictogenic metaphors as a manifestation of speech aggression

The notion of a conflictogenic metaphor is in the process of establishing itself in linguistics. To date, scholars perceive the term as hyperonymic because of the large number of conceptual metaphors that contextually feature as a means of explicit or even implicit speech aggression with the primary aim of humiliating, discrediting or even demonizing political opponents. Based on his research of a large corpus of texts of political discourse, Anatoliy Baranov, the leading Russian expert in the field of political metaphorology, came to the conclusion that in parallel with the growing crisis situation (political, economic, national) and the deepening of social tensions in society, the number of conflictogenic metaphors was also increasing, which could serve as a kind of "linguistic litmus test" pointing to the unfavourable situation in society.[216] These are primarily metaphorical models with conceptual vectors of aggression (military and criminal metaphors), metaphors of deviation from the natural course of things (morbial metaphors), metaphors pointing to the improbability of events (theatrical metaphors), to material calculation (financial metaphors), zoomorphic metaphors (pig, dog, ram, donkey, hyena, snake), anthropomorphic metaphors (mostly physiological: sexual metaphors – sexual organs, sexual perversion, promiscuity), bestial metaphors (Satan, the devil, the beast) and destructive metaphors (natural cataclysms, catastrophes, disintegration, decay, devastation, etc.).[217]

The tendency of increasing speech aggression through the metaphorization of discourse was not only noticed by Russian researchers, but also by the German political scientist Frank Decker. In the process of analysing the language of populism, he concludes that one of the current communication strategies is "the use of biological and violent metaphors, the language of cruelty and war. The rejection of all that is alien and 'unnatural' is often expressed through biological formulations designed to portray an image of a sick society threatened by decay and disintegration. This corresponds to the frequent use of sexual, medical, or animal metaphors."[218]

---

216   Baranov, A. (2000). Metafory v politicheskom diskurse: jazykovye markery krizisnosti politicheskoj situacii. In L. Zybatow (Ed.), *Linguistic Change in Europe: 1990–2000*, (pp. 35–42). Wien: Peter Lang.

217   Cingerová & Dulebová, 2019, p. 113.

218   Decker, F. (2004). *Der neue Rechtspopulismus*. Opladen: Leske + Budrich.

The intentions of metaphorical aggression are explicit. It visibly becomes a "tool for disqualifying the opponent, for populists are always looking for an enemy and often justify political decisions by their efforts to defeat an enemy (often fictitious) ... and this is a compelling reason to use securitization vocabulary based on the alleged "danger.""[219]

4.2 Conflictogenic metaphors in the Facebook posts of Robert Fico

In the process of an extensive and precise analysis of the language and communication strategies of the representatives of radical populism, several key strategies have been identified. They include, "a dichotomous perception of reality in the sense of US and THEM, THE OTHERS, or THE STRANGERS, depending on the vertical or horizontal perception of the enemies".[220] This research into Fico's securitizing speech acts (published on his Facebook page in 2022) fully confirms this idea, as absolutely all of the metaphors with strongly negative semantics that we extracted refer to the Smer party's real or alleged political "enemies", whose activities allegedly create the aforementioned "threats" to the referent objects (threatened entities). Other distinctive speech strategies include the use of hyperbolic means of expression (in the idiolect of Fico, especially in the case of negativizing adjectives such as the *vagabond* minister Mikulec, the *treasonous* treaty with the USA, the *enormous* debt, the *godforsaken* sacrilege, the *monstrous* theatre), but also "dramatization, scandalization, incitement of negative emotions; eliciting a sense of threat and fear; appealing to emotions such as anger and indignation, whether justified or not" (Ibidem), while "one way of dramatizing the situation and emphasizing the threat motif is to use words from the military vocabulary associated with a feeling of being threatened by an external or internal enemy."[221]

The war metaphor is exceptionally frequent in Fico's writing:

SL → *celé mesiace v parlamente **vojnoví štváči rinčia zbraňami** / vo svojej **svätej vojne** proti opozícii ho ústava a zákony nezaujímajú / **Rusko vyhráva** globálnu finančnú a ekonomickú **vojnu** otvorenú Bidenom a európskymi spojencami / Takíto **vojnoví štváči** ako Čaputová a Heger privedú Slovensko do nešťastia / **parlamentne vojny** nás vyjdú draho / **chceli vojnu**...budú ju mať / sme jasne protifašistickí a odmietame **vojnových***

---

219   Štefančík, R. (2022). *Radikálny populizmus v ére pandémie COVID-19 a vojny na Ukrajine*. Bratislava: Ekonóm.

220   Štefančík, 2022, p. 184.

221   Štefančík, 2022, p. 125.

*štváčov Čaputovú a spol./ z nášho územia vytvorí **potenciálny terč** / tešiť sa z toho, že sme tým Rusko **strelili do kolien** pričom si neuvedomiť, že sami sme si **strelili do hlavy.***[222]

Similar to war metaphors, the feeling of threat is also evoked by criminal metaphors. In the process of their abundant use, Fico demonstrates linguistic creativity:

SL → *si zobrali Slovákov za **rukojemníkov** vlastných sporov / organizovaná **zločinecká skupina** novinárov útočí na štátne inštitúcie / **ekonomická vražda** občanov Slovenska a slovenskej ekonomiky / časť **výpalného** mala ísť vtedajšiemu ministrovi financií E. Hegerovi / budú niesť zodpovednosť za svoje **zločiny** / Na rozdiel od Hegera nikdy **som nekšeftoval** so slovenskou suverenitou a slovenskými národnými záujmami / Heger je tak stratený, že sa do toho všetkého nechal namočiť a stal sa **spolupáchateľ** / to, čo vychádza na povrch, je už skutočný **humus** nezákonnosti / podľa Hegera každý, kto má iný názor ako ukrajinský prezident, je **zločinec** / D. Lipšic by nemal byť prokurátorom, ale **šéfom spolku** najbezcharakternejších ľudí a **podvodníkov** / Vyšetrovatelia korupčných prípadov sú „**lumpi**".*[223]

He likes to use strongly negative and intimidating morbial metaphors (deviations from the natural course of things, diseases, their symptoms, etc.), mostly in an attempt to point out the incompetence of the current government and to ironize its particular representatives:

---

222 EL → for months in the parliament, **the warmongers have been rattling their weapons** / in his **holy war** against the opposition, he doesn't care about the constitution and the law / **Russia is winning** the global financial and economic **war** started by Biden and European allies / Such **warmongers** as Caputova and Heger will lead Slovakia into disaster / **parliamentary wars** will cost us dearly / **they wanted war**…they will have it / we are clearly anti-fascist and reject the **warmongers** Čaputová and co. / our territory will make **a potential target** / rejoice in the fact that we **have shot** Russia **in the knees** and not realize that we **have shot** ourselves **in the head.**

223 EL → have taken Slovaks **hostage** in their own controversies / organized **criminal group** of journalists attacking state institutions / **economic murder** of Slovak citizens and the Slovak economy / part of the **ransom** should have gone to the then Minister of Finance E. Heger / will be held accountable for their **crimes** / Unlike Heger, I have **never traded** in Slovak sovereignty and Slovak national interests / Heger is so lost that he got dragged into all this and became **complicit** / what is coming to light is already a real **mess** of illegality / according to Heger, anyone who has a different opinion than the Ukrainian president is **a criminal** / D. Lipšic should not be a prosecutor, but **the head of an association of** the most unprincipled people and **crooks** / Investigators of corruption cases are "**crooks**".

SL → *Vláda je v **klinickej smrti**, neschopná prijímať rozhodnutia na pomoc Slovákom v
kríze / Máme neexistujúceho premiéra, **duševne chorého** ministra financií a rozhádanú
koalíciu / vďaka krytiu Lipšica a Matoviča **zbláznili** z moci / predsedom vlády a ministrom
financií SR v rokoch 2020 – 2022 bol obyčajný **magor** / skutočnou hlavou celej vlády je
daňový podvodník a **psychiatrický pacient** / požadujeme, aby v situácii, keď **magor múti
vodu**, okamžite vyhlásila referendum / Takto si predstavuje "spravodlivosť" **psychopat** so
svojimi kumpánmi / Sú to čistí **blázni a sadisti**, ktorí sa vyžívajú v zatváraní ľudí bez
dôvodov / nech už ani len neuvažuje o podpore tohto **verejného blázinca** / Slovensku
vládnu **duchovní bezdomovci**, ktorí ignorujú našu históriu/ sankčne šialenstvo sa šíri ako
rakovina po svete.*[224]

As an experienced securitization actor, Fico is keen on using the impressive
and frightening morbial metaphor of *suicide* in the process of thematizing the
dangers that allegedly threaten our economy, which cannot fail to arouse fear in
his numerous followers on Facebook and followers in real life:

SL → *ak sankcie proti Rusku devastujú životnú úroveň Slovákov, tak to nie sú sankcie
proti Rusku, ale **ekonomická samovražda** / to nie sú sankcie proti Rusku, ale **ekonomická
samovražda**, za ktorú Heger poslušne zdvihol ruku / Odstavenie dodávok ruskej ropy je
ekonomická samovražda.*[225]

However, in his view, there is a way to eliminate these "threats" to Slovakia. It is
articulated through a morbial metaphor again:

---

224   EL → The government is in a condition of **clinical death**, unable to take decisions
      to help Slovaks in crisis / We have a non-existent prime minister, a **mentally
      ill** finance minister and a fractured coalition / thanks to the cover of Lipšic
      and Matovič, they went insane with power / the Prime Minister and Minister
      of Finance of the Slovak Republic in 2020–2022 was a common **lunatic** / the
      real head of the entire government is a tax fraud and **a psychiatric patient** / we
      demand that the President immediately call a referendum in a situation where **a
      lunatic is muddying the waters** (literal translation of a Slovak phraseme which
      means *to plan/organize unfair or illegal actions*, note of the authors) / This is how **a
      psychopath** and his cronies imagine "justice" / They are sheer **lunatics and sadists**
      who thrive on locking people up for no reason at all / let her not even consider
      supporting this **public madhouse** / Slovakia is ruled by **the spiritual homeless**
      who ignore our history / sanctioned madness is spreading like a **cancer** around
      the world.

225   EL → if sanctions against Russia devastate the standard of living of Slovaks, it is not
      sanctions against Russia, but **economic suicide** / it's not sanctions against Russia, it's
      economic suicide, for which Heger obediently raised his hand / Cutting off supplies
      of Russian oil is **economic suicide**.

SL → *len predčasne voľby môžu* **vyprášiť infantilných** *politikov a* **psychiatrických pacientov** *od kormidla Slovenska.*[226]

And it was pre-term elections that at that time represented the main, broadly-declared goal of the securitization process (which ultimately proved successful).

He uses the metaphor of children as a negative and demeaning (belittling) one, which in a different context is not inherently a manifestation of speech aggression, but in the discourse strategies of the former long-serving prime minister it sounds conflictogenic (quite often it is an absolutely incorrect comparison to fools and small children, the supposed pragmatic effect of which is to portray the opponents as incompetent, intellectually and socially immature, inexperienced, or inept individuals):

> SL → *dostanú k moci* **malé decká a blázni** / **Malé decká** *po chvíli* **pustia do nohavíc** *a ujdú a* **blázni sa tešia**, *že môžu dokončiť rozvrat štátu do dokonalosti / bezprecedentnej vládnej krízy spôsobenej* **malými politickými deckami** / *Gratulujem, pán Sulík k Vášmu* **ďalšiemu detskému politickému výkonu** /na tribúne odporu **voči bláznom a malým deckám** *vo vláde.*[227]

According to our observations to date, the metaphorical concept of "theatre" has an implicitly conflictual nature whenever it operates as a metaphorical projection of events of a political and social nature.[228] It is particularly widespread in political domains of communication, while "the pragmatic potential of this metaphorical model is determined by the pronounced conceptual vector of insincerity, artificiality, unnaturalness, imitation of reality: political actors are not living real lives and are following someone else's plans instead of their own will",[229] or they deliberately dramatize events, exaggerate, deceive and act theatrically in an attempt to impress the recipient.[230] These are extremely popular and semantically negative linguoculturemes in the Slovak linguistic image of the

---

226   EL → only pre-term elections can **drive infantile** politicians and **psychiatric patients away** from the steering wheel of Slovakia.

227   EL → **little kids and fools** get into power / **Little kids will wet their pants** and run away after a while and **fools are happy** to complete the disintegration of the state to perfection / unprecedented government crisis caused by **small political children** / Congratulations, Mr. Sulík on your next **childish political performance** / on the podium of resistance **to fools and small children** in the government

228   Dulebová & Krajčovičová, 2020, p. 21.

229   Chudinov, A. (2013). *Očerki po sovremennoj političeskoj metaforologii.* Jekaterinburg: UGPU, p. 79.

230   Spišiaková, M., & Mocková, N. (2022). Colours in politics in Spanish speaking countries. *Folia Linguistica et Litteraria: Časopis za nauku o jeziku i književnosti, 39,* 273–294.

world "based on the unity of linguistic and extra-linguistic reality, characterized by a rich ethno-cultural expressive value in the national or universal linguistic-cultural community."[231] Among the favourite slots of the concept of *theatre* in 2022 in Fico's speech acts were the words *circus* and *farce* (both of which have an explicitly ironic nature, and are employed as expressive denominations for *confusion, bustle, madhouse,* and *tragicomic, humiliating action*, respectively):

> SL → *Referendum je príležitosť pre obce, ktoré sa stali obeťou Matovičových **cirkusových čísiel** za viac ako miliardu / **Trestnoprávny cirkus** má za úlohu len jediné, prekryť nemohúcnosť Hegerovej vlády / Koaličné **Humberto** pokračuje / Správa Európskej komisie o stave právneho štátu na Slovensku je **fraška** / toto nie je vládna kríza, ale **fraška** / celá záležitosť je politický proces a **fraška** / Slovenská politika sa zmenila na **absurdnú frašku**.[232]*

However, even the seemingly semantically neutral term "theatre" has a distinctly negative connotation in the politician's idiolect due to its repulsive adjectives:

> SL → *Hrá sa tu jedno **obludné divadlo**, opozičné a mediálne /Je to **zúfalé politické divadlo** Matoviča, Hegera a Čaputovej / Je to **trápne divadlo** zradcov.[233]*

Financial metaphors have also become a means of speech aggression when they point to material calculation, profiteering, fraud or obscuring real goals:

> SL → *Nápad prezidentky Čaputovej vypnúť rusky plyn je jasnou **biznisprihrávkou pre USA**, ktorú si dnes nemôžeme dovoliť! / Z. Čaputová, E. Heger či I. Korčok sa v poslednej dobe správajú viac ako **obchodní zástupcovia amerických ropných firiem** než zástupcovia slovenských národných záujmov / vláda zatúžila po **kšefte** a zhrabla Jackpot.[234]*

---

231 Zahorák, A. (2022). *Precedentné fenomény ako nástroj v interpretácii prekladového umeleckého textu.* Nitra: Univerzita Konštantína Filozofa v Nitre.

232 EL → The referendum is an opportunity for the municipalities that have fallen victim to Matovič's **circus tricks** for over a billion / **The circus of criminal proceedings** has only one task, to cover up the impotence of Heger's government / / The coalition's **Humberto** circus continues / The European Commission's report on the state of the rule of law in Slovakia is **a farce** / this is not a government crisis, but **a farce** / the whole thing is a political process and **a farce** / Slovak politics has turned into **an absurd farce**.

233 EL → There is **a hideous theatre** – opposition and media – being played out here / It is **a desperate political theatre** of Matovič, Heger and Čaputová / It is **an embarrassing theatre** of traitors.

234 EL → President Čaputová's idea to shut off Russian gas is a clear **business pass to the U.S.** that we cannot afford today! / Z. Čaputová, E. Heger or I. Korčok have recently been behaving more like **sales representatives of American oil companies** than representatives of Slovak national interests / the government was hungry for **a business deal** and grabbed the jackpot.

Traditionally, zoomorphic metaphors are particularly offensive and aggressive. The use of terms from the animal world is significantly dehumanizing and sometimes highly invective. Interestingly, Fico applies the metaphor of rams in the discourse opposition WE/US-THEY/THEM predominantly to the otherwise positive WE/US in the sense of "let's not be rams", which, however, can be seen as a sophisticated speech strategy aimed at evoking a close relationship with its recipients, so intimate that one can afford to speak directly[235]:

> SL → *Ako u debilov,* **tvárime sa ako barani,** *že nemôžeme nič povedať / Ako* **hlúpi barani** *sledujeme americké záujmy na Ukrajine a poškodzujeme sa / stále sú v Európskej únii lídri, ktorí majú na to iný názor, a ktorí,* **nie ako barani,** *automaticky súhlasia s tým, čo hovoria Spojené štáty americké / chceme byť solidárni hráči, ale to neznamená, že* **pôjdeme ako barani na bitúnok.**[236]

However, he "honours" his political enemies with much more expressive animal metaphors:

> SL → *Takýto potápajúci sa koráb a* **utekajúce potkany** *si ľudia nezaslúžia! / Ste* **utekajúce potkany!** *Váš koráb sa už potápa! / Matovič sa* **schoval ako potkan,** *musíme desať dní počkať / Matovičov* **pes Lipšic** *dnes opäť* **zaštekal** */ Stali sa z nich* **cynické zvieratá** */ Pán minister vnútra Mikulec,* **na NAKA máte zvieratá,** *to nie sú ľudia.*[237]

After all, for a politician who is infamous for calling journalists *stupid hyenas, slithery snakes, toilet spiders* or *intrusive insects* even during his time in government, it cannot be surprising that he is "toughening up" his rhetoric in his precarious place in the opposition.

He is fond of using conflictogenic metaphors of disintegration and natural cataclysms not only in the process of stigmatizing political rivals and scorning the current state of the political scene (*only ruins are left of the government*), but also as a figurative appeal for the necessity of immediate action:

---

235 Hirschová, M. *Pragmatika v češtine.* Praha: Karolinum, 2013, s. 231.

236 EL → Like morons, we **pretend like rams** that we can't say anything / Like **stupid rams,** we pursue American interests in Ukraine and do harm to ourselves / there are still leaders in the European Union who have a different view on this and who, **not like rams,** automatically agree with what the United States of America says / we want to be solidarity players, but that does not mean that we will go **like rams to the slaughterhouse.**

237 EL → People don't deserve such a sinking ship and **escaping rats!** / You are **runaway rats!** Your ship is already sinking! / Matovič **hid like a rat,** we have to wait ten days / Matovič's **dog Lipšic barked** again today / They have become **cynical animals** / Minister of the Interior Mikulec, you have **animals in NAKA,** they are not humans.

SL → *lokálne búrky to je málo,* **musí prísť veľké ľudové tornádo** *žeby tato vláda odišla.*[238]

The goal of securitization is thus presented metaphorically, figuratively, but explicitly and suggestively enough.

4.3 Colloquial phrasemes as a tool of speech aggression

One of the populists' communication strategies is "referring to the will of the people; the people as a central category; referring to common sense."[239] Thus, populists also often base the imagery of their speech acts on colloquial phrases, whose use fully corresponds to the discursive strategy *one of you – to my folks.*

Phrasemes have a distinct metaphorical nature, and both imagery and a certain persuasive effect associated with it. "The basic feature of a phrase is, first of all, its metaphoricity, the obligatory presence of connotations, as well as its generally widespread use and familiarity among language users [...] metaphorical denominations (phraseological units) are emotionally charged, expressive, markedly evaluative [...] Concise, pithy, accurate evaluations of a person and a situation are achieved with the help of established images of a metaphorical type, i.e., with the help of phrasemes".[240]

Our research corpus has convincingly illustrated the fact that Robert Fico rarely turns to complex historical or literary allusions in the process of securitization. Apparently, he does not assume that they will be understood by his followers. In this he is right, since, for example, the precedent-setting expression of literary origin used by him in August 2022, "and now that the liberals are going to make strong state interventions, something is rotten in the state of Denmark",[241] several of the numerous commentators subsequently expressed puzzlement as to why Denmark was mentioned when the speech was dedicated to Slovakia.

On the phraseological axis of *bookishness – colloquiality*, colloquial phrases are no doubt more expressive and "immediately appealing", which is why Fico logically prefers these often highly offensive phrases, the use of which effectively

---

238   EL → local storms are not enough, there **must be a great national tornado** for this government to leave.

239   Štefančík, 2022, p. 184.

240   Ďurčo, P. et al. (1995). *Frazeologická terminológia.* SAV. https://www.juls.savba.sk/ ediela/frazeologicka_terminologia/

241   Smer-SD (2022, August 25). R. Fico: slovalcu aj Duslu Šaľa by sa dalo rýchlo pomôcť zdanením bánk, R. Sulík to odmieta. Veci verejné. https://veci-verejne.sk/r-fico-slovalcu-aj-duslu-sala-by-sa-dalo-rychlo-pomoct-zdanenim-bank-r-sulik-to-odmi eta%EF%BF%BC/

stylizes him as "our man" and "the right man" who can speak the language of the common people and trusts only a man's word and a proper handshake:

SL → *Vlada **kašle na** vlastných občanov / Ľudia si môžu "**hodiť slučku**", lebo takto ich ekonomicky v histórii Slovenska ešte nikto nepoškodil / Demokracia a sloboda prejavu **dostáva** na Slovensku **na frak** ako nikdy a nikde / Proti zdražovaniu na Slovensku **ste urobili veľké**.... / Sulík sa stratil v politike ako **Maďar v kukurici** / Keby otcovia SNP videli dnešné Slovensko, **obracali by sa v hrobe**! / Sorosovi novinári idú **vybuchnúť od jedu** a vláda ma chce zatvoriť. Sloboda prejavu prestala u nás existovať a liberálna demokracia **ukazuje svoju pravú tvár** / Ako si kapry dobrovoľne **nevypustia svoj rybník**, ani poslanci vládnej koalície si neskrátia volebne obdobie / Čakajú nás **krušné chvíle**, lebo slovenská vláda je vo vojenskej podpore Ukrajiny ako **odtrhnutá z reťaze** / **Robia** z GP M. Žilinku **dobrý deň** / Ale **príde** aj na tohto Matovičovho **psa mráz** / Slovensko je mesiace **kŕmené klamstvami** o vojne na Ukrajine / Nech už **má Boha pri sebe** a vypadne.[242]*

As can be seen from the above examples, only the phrases *krušné chvíle* (translated as *a tough time*), *ukazovať pravú tvár* (translated as *to show the true face*) and *obracať sa v hrobe* (translated as *to turn in their graves*) have a bookish character, all of them with distinctly negative semantics as well. In other cases, Fico uses colloquial or even vulgar phrasemes (he even uses the phrase *urobiť veľké hovno* [literal translation: *to do shit* which means to do nothing at all] where the last word is replaced with dots, but it still does not diminish its invective nature, as every Slovak knows it and immediately replaces the dots with the "right word" in his/her mind). Particularly frightening is the phraseme *hodiť si slučku* (translated as *to throw a noose around the neck*), which is a metaphor for

---

242   EL → The government **doesn't give a damn** about its own citizens / People can "**throw a noose** around their necks" because nobody in the history of Slovakia has ever harmed them economically like this / Democracy and freedom of speech **are getting hammered** in Slovakia like never before and nowhere else / You **have done**.... against price increase in Slovakia / Sulík got lost in politics **like a Hungarian in corn** / If the fathers of the SNP (Slovak National Uprising of 1944, authors' note) had seen today's Slovakia, they would **turn in their graves**! / Soros's journalists are going to **explode out of fury** and the government wants to shut me down. Freedom of speech has ceased to exist in our country and liberal democracy is **showing its true face** / Just as carp **do not voluntarily drain their pond**, neither do the members of the ruling coalition shorten their term of office / We are in for **a tough time**, because the Slovak government acts like it's **cut loose from a chain** in its military support of Ukraine / They are "making a good day" (literal translation of a Slovak phraseme which means: to poke fun of sb./st., authors' note) out of Prosecutor General M. Žilinka / But the **frost will come to** this **dog** of Matovič's too / Slovakia has been **fed with lies** about the war in Ukraine for months / Let him **have God on his side** and get out of here.

a cruel suicide and evokes a sense of helplessness in the recipient. The phraseme *Maďar v kukurici* (literal translation: *Hungarian in corn*) is a manifestation of his absolute political incorrectness (for a man who otherwise likes to mention the common interests of the V4 in the European space and appeals to the necessity of common strategies). However, the desire to impress potential voters with a phraseme with great pejorative and ironic potential outweighs the arguments of reason and decency, probably also because the politician does not perceive the Hungarian national minority in Slovakia as his potential voters.

4.4 Historical and political metaphors with markedly negative semantics

In the process of securitization, Fico turns to stereotypical images (referring to notorious names and facts of history), while not avoiding instrumentalizing history (especially in the case of events and names associated with the glorified "big Russian brother" and the idea of Slavic mutuality). Clearly the most frequently used metaphorical conceptual scheme (frame) is fascism (it corresponds with some thematically correlated slots such as Gestapo, Nazis, Hitler, etc.):

> SL → *vyšetrovatelia a prokurátori sú takí sadisti, od ktorých by sa mohlo učiť aj neslávne* **nacistické gestapo** / *fašisticky vydieral policajta* / *je to obyčajné* **fašistické svinstvo** /*Ak by bol na Slovensku trest smrti, tak nás títo blázni za politickú prácu povešajú, ako v 30. rokoch* **v nacistickom Nemecku!** / **Gestapácky kabát** *posielame odtiaľto zo Smeru pánovi Repovi lebo je to* **gestapák** / *Naposledy s takouto vervou obhajovali vojnu istí* **Adolf & Benito**.[243]

Fico's discourse confirms what our previous research on the rhetoric of the populist left has already indicated (see Dulebová, 2021),[244] namely, that the purposeful instrumentalization of history is accompanied by a reinterpretation of ideologemes, and thus fascism, even in Fico's securitizing rhetoric, semantically corresponds to everything that does not suit his political intentions. This leads to the ideological disorientation of Slovak society, the essence of which was

---

243 EL → investigators and prosecutors are the kind of sadists that even the infamous **Nazi Gestapo** could learn from / blackmailing a policeman **fascist style** / it's just plain **fascist filth** / If there was a death penalty in Slovakia, these fools would hang us for our political work, as in **Nazi Germany** in the 1930s! / We're sending a **Gestapo coat** to Mr. Repa from here, from Smer, because he is **a Gestapo man** / The last time war was defended with such vehemence by a certain **Adolf & Benito**.

244 Dulebová, I. (2021). Metaforizácia vakcinácie pri jej sekuritizácii v slovenskom politickom diskurze In R. Štefančík (Ed.), *Jazyk a politika: na pomedzí lingvistiky a politológie VI* (pp. 49–60). Bratislava: Ekonóm.

summed up by former Slovak Foreign Minister Rastislav Kačer in his Facebook post (30 August 2023): "Looking at the alternative celebrations of the Slovak National Uprising in Zvolen, one is painfully aware of the catastrophic condition of our society. The collective schizophrenia is almost absurd. Next to a communist there is a neo-Nazi. First a Guardsman,[245] then a Communist, then a confirmed Catholic. Loving our holy President Tiso,[246] at the same time glorifying the Soviet Union, celebrating communism… This is neither normal nor acceptable by anyone with a minimum of education, morals and character. And common sense".[247] Nevertheless, the securitization process is not about common sense. It is about common sense clouded by fear and hatred.

The high frequency of the use of some politemes in their figurative meaning leads to the fact that they gradually lose their figurativeness in political discourse, but at the same time acquire new connotations and a new axiological dimension. For example, the formerly semantically-neutral politeme *liberalism* is demonized in various (often unexpected) contexts and becomes by far the most commonly used curse word in the discourse of Slovak political populists and extremists. How *genocide* (the mass murder of a population; a crime against humanity) can be *economic* is also not explained; its contextual involvement becomes literally limitless, and the metaphor of *lynching* loses its original content altogether and is subsumed into the synonymic line of *insulting/hurting*:

SL → *ekonomická* **genocída** *vlastného národa / nás budú za takúto slovenskú socialno – demokratickú politiku* **lynčovať** *slovenské* **liberálne** *médiá a každý, kto nemá rád Slovensko.*[248]

Also surprising for the securitizing speech tactics of a leftist radical are the references ironizing the representatives and symbols of communist ideology:

SL → *dnes to D. Lipšic robí lepšie ako* **najzarytejší komunistickí prokurátori** *v minulom storočí / Je to bezcharakterný* **aparátčik** */* **ŠTBáci** *sa pri politických procesoch snažili zachovať aspoň formu.*[249]

---

245   Referring to the National Guard of the fascist Slovak State, 1939–1945.
246   Roman Catholic priest who was president of the Slovak State (1939–1945) collaborating with Nazi Germany.
247   Kačer, R. (2023). Facebook. https://www.facebook.com/rastislav.kacer
248   EL → economic **genocide** of our own nation / we will **be lynched** for such Slovak social-democratic policy by the Slovak **liberal** media and everyone who doesn't like Slovakia.
249   EL → Today D. Lipšic does it better than the most **die-hard communist** prosecutors in the last century / He is a spineless **apparatchik** / In political trials, the **communist security agency** tried to preserve at least some decorum.

Of course, Fico's securitization tactics must not overlook the name of George Soros, which has long been a universal name symbolizing abstract and absolute "external" evil in the discourse strategies of Slovak populists:

> SL → **Sorosova črieda prasiat** v denníku SME *likviduje demokraciu* / *Na Slovensku pôsobí* **Sorošova črieda prasiat** / *Z. Čaputová, podobne ako A. Kiska, je len jeden z ďalších* **výplodov sorosovskej fantázie** / *Žena, ktorá je schopná do bodky napĺňať* **sny sorosových mimovládiek** / *Mali sme pravdu,* **Sorosove peniaze** *ovplyvňujú dianie na Slovensku* / *MDIF je pod kontrolou* **jedného z najväčších podvodníkov na svete Georga Sorosa.**[250]

Uttering the name of Soros becomes an "unquestionable" argument in the struggle of left-wing radicals with liberals, NGOs, NATO, President Čaputová and other "anti-Slovak elements". In the process of analysing our research corpus, we noticed that so-called non-deductive arguments, namely "referring to experts, witnesses, and arguments ad populum (commonly held beliefs) when the community's attitude is presented as a reason in favour of the truthfulness of the claim"[251] are used by political populists with gusto. The constant repetition of the name Soros in a negative context makes a certain (significant) part of Slovak society uncritically adopt the idea of his "harmfulness" and thus gradually this anthroponym becomes an "unquestionable" argument ad populum (because "everyone knows" who Soros is).

As demonstrated by all of the examples above, the dominant functions of the various forms of metaphorization in Robert Fico's securitization statuses are primarily persuasive, axiological, expressive and modelling. On the surface, the expressive function (the immediate impact on the recipient's emotions) rises to the fore, but no less important is the modelling function, which shapes the ideas of the securitized referent objects and the "dangers" threatening them, as well as his own role as a "saviour", into a specific image of the world that fully corresponds with his intentions. The persuasive function manifests itself in an attempt to influence the addressees (to induce a sense of imminent danger), and to shift their political opinions and, subsequently, voting decisions. The axiological function manifests itself in the creation of a system of values for

---

250   EL → **Soros's herd of pigs** in the SME daily is liquidating democracy / **Soros's herd of pigs** is operating in Slovakia / Z. Čaputová, like A. Kiska, is just another **product of Soros's imagination** / A woman who can fulfil the **dreams of Soros's NGOs** to the full / We were right, **Soros's money** is influencing events in Slovakia / MDIF is under the control of **one of the biggest crooks in the world, George Soros.**

251   Zouhar, M. (2022). *Argument: nástroj myslenia a presviedčania.* Bratislava: VEDA SAV, p. 129.

the recipient, advantageous for Fico as the actor of securitization (through an unambiguous and unidirectional, figurative evaluation).

Very much in line with our reflections and conclusions of the analysis of the selection and use of metaphors by Robert Fico are the observations of Zuzana Zimenová, who states that "the metaphors that Robert Fico is so fond of using are not just a passive ornament of his speech, since people naturally tend to use metaphors that correspond to their value setting, perspective, and experience. In short, we particularly like those metaphors that reflect our own mental world. If we want to explain something to someone in a simplified way by means of a metaphor, we usually reach for one that refers to images that are familiar to us, that "suit" our nature. They offer simplifications through which one can easily grasp the essence. But they also capture the essence of the author. There is a famous statement of his (concerning the break-up of a party) that when a brothel does not work, it is the girls who need to be replaced, not the beds. To liken a political party to a brothel and its members to girls is simplistic to the extreme... Obscene metaphors, sexual innuendos, dirty jokes – this is the mental world of a man who suddenly installs himself in the role of a defender of democracy, human rights and liberties, justice and decency."[252]

When the democratic values of Slovak society, the values of the rule of law and the welfare state, the standard of living of Slovaks, or even the independence, sovereignty and statehood of Slovakia become referent objects in the process of securitization, it is meant to present them as threatened: the values must be unconditionally defended, even at the cost of transgressing the standard "rules of the game". As we sought to illustrate in our research, a compelling metaphor targeted at a specific group of voters is an effective tool for the success of a given process.

The securitization process we have been monitoring can be assessed as successful, since at the end of August 2022, in the Presidential Palace, representatives of Smer-SD sumitted more than 406,039 signatures for a referendum on the dissolution of the government and changes to the Constitution of the Slovak Republic, as a result of which the President finally announced a referendum on pre-term elections. Almost half a million people came to believe the threats articulated by the influential securitization actor, the experienced politician R. Fico.

---

252 Zimenová, Z. (2019, January 10). O bordeli, dievčatách a posteliach alebo keď hrubosť formuje realitu. *Blog Sme.* https://dennikn.sk/blog/1345949/o-bordeli-die vcatach-a-posteliach-alebo-ked-hrubost-formuje-realitu

In his securitization tactics (constructing threats and then demonstrating how he and his party will be able to eliminate them), Fico successfully advances even further, as evidenced by the pre-election voter preferences for the parliamentary elections of 30 September 2023, in which the SMER-SD party led by Fico has the highest preference (over 20 %). In this context, one has to agree with the view that "in a pluralist democracy, political actors compete, which forces them to apply methods and means of communication that will help them succeed. Practice shows that strict adherence to the codified linguistic standard is not a significant prerequisite for success in this battle (although linguistic "transgressions" are being pointed out in public linguistic criticism). More relevant for the moral advancement of society is the question regarding the consequences of the modes of communication and communication practices in this competitive space for the future of society. It is a question of communication culture and its critique with regard to the cultivation of society."[253] However, Fico is completely uninterested in the issue of moral development of society and society's communication cultivation (as is evident from our examples). He is concerned with winning elections, seizing power, eliminating political opponents. And when he finally succeeds, it will be interesting to observe the subsequent process of desecuritization (in the introductory chapter we have already discussed it using the example of the 2016 parliamentary elections, in which, after winning, he immediately forgot about the major pre-election theme of the alleged "danger of migrants" for Slovakia).

Securitization "here and now" with the help of sophisticated speech acts (involving impressive conflictogenic metaphors) is the shortest and surest way to increase the number of his supporters and to achieve his political goals. His well-conceived and "punchy" social networking strategy helps him significantly, which is also confirmed by Gabriel Tóth, a communications expert from New School Communications, who notes that "Robert Fico has long been one of the most successful politicians on social networks. Firstly, in terms of content, which is sufficiently controversial and thus has gained interaction. At the same time, he also helps himself with paid advertising. His numbers have been good for a long time and in recent months he has risen even more compared to other politicians; the Smer-SD party is also significantly dominant the category of the most successful political party on Facebook."[254]

---

253 Dolník, 2020, p. 12.
254 Tóth, G. (2023, Febuary 19). Smer vie, ako na to! Fico suverénne ovládol sociálne siete, Matovičovi ostanú len oči pre plač. *Plus 1 Deň*. https://www1.pluska.sk/spravy/z-domova/smer-vie-ako-to-fico-suverenne-ovladol-socialne-siete-matovicovi-ostanu-len-oci-pre-plac

Nowadays, social networks such as Facebook, TikTok and Instagram are among the key communication channels of politicians, political parties and movements, reaching hundreds of thousands of potential voters through them, and, especially on Facebook, it is the politicians who "work with negative content, sometimes even with controversial and extremist" issues, who become successful, emphasizing pressing topics, connected with concerns about various aspects of everyday existence.

Raising as much fear as possible (including through negative metaphorization) and then playing political games by manipulating the fears of the voters is a strategy that bears fruit today. It is no coincidence that paragraph 22 of the document entitled *Security Strategy of the Slovak Republic 2021* states that "the number and scale of subversive and coercive activities of various actors using disinformation and propaganda to disrupt or manipulate decision-making mechanisms in the state, to influence public opinion in their favour and to destabilize the political situation is increasing [...] The public is exposed to the increasing spread of disinformation and conspiracy theories that can threaten human health, disrupt social cohesion and provoke public violence and social unrest."[255]

In the contemporary world of Slovak politics (which is increasingly becoming an online world), a metaphor is an effective weapon in the hands of an actor who has no moral inhibitions. This is also happening because the online world has blurred the line "between criticism and abuse, between argument and quarrel, between smoothness and vulgarity, between logic and faith or intuition [...] Authenticity and freedom of speech without accountability have become essential tools of an all-popular pseudo-argumentation that claims the status of public acceptance and true knowledge."[256] And so metaphorical-insults, metaphorical-quarrels, metaphorical-vulgarisms and metaphorical-pseudo-arguments have come to the fore. In the vein of contemporary political Machiavellianism, *the ends justify the means*. And the metaphor, as it turns out, is one of the most powerful means to the end – securitization.

---

255   Ministry of Defence of the Slovak Republic (2021). *Security Strategy of the Slovak Republic.* https://www.mosr.sk/data/files/4263_210128-bezpecnostna-strategia-sr-2021.pdf

256   Sámelová, 2022, p. 7.

V. Securitization of International Migration in Slovak Political Discourse

In this part of the text, we will outline how the topic of international migration is securitized in Slovak political discourse. The securitization of migration in the global context arose after the attacks on civilian targets in the USA on 11 September 2001, but its origins can be observed much earlier in European political discourses.[257] According to Karyotis,[258] the origins of the securitization of migration in Western Europe can be traced back to the 1970s, in migration policymaking influenced by security factors, thus, long before the appearance of the first anti-immigration political parties. Since the 1980s, some political parties have increasingly articulated concerns about illegal migrants, cheap labour from abroad, welfare recipients and even terrorists and Islamists. It was specifically the Copenhagen School that provided the theoretical framework for exploring the relationship between international migration and securitization.[259] The Copenhagen School is grounded in the argument that we should analyse the process by which actors construct problems as threats to security, rather than focussing on security as something that exists.[260] In particular, migration and migrants are often presented by political elites as a threat to internal security, although this argument is primarily used by politicians to mobilize voters, rather than to seek solutions to potential problems associated with migration processes.

Ceyhan and Tsoukala[261] note that the rhetorical arguments are similar in almost all anti-immigration discourses. As a rule, they are formulated around four basic axes: socioeconomic, securitarian, identitarian and political. The

257 Huysmans, J. (2000). Contested community: Migration and the question of the political in the EU. In M. Kelstrup, & M. C. Williams (Eds.), *International Relations Theory and the Politics of European Integration. Power, Security and Community* (pp. 149–170). London, New York: Routledge.

258 Karyotis, G. (2007). European migration policy in the aftermath of September 2001. The security – migration nexus. *Innovation, 20*(1), 1–17.

259 Demirkol, A. (2023). A perspective on critical security concept and international migration Nexus through Copenhagen School: The quest for societal security. *Lectio Socialis, 7*(1), 1–10.

260 Karyotis, 2007.

261 Ceyhan, A., & Tsoukala, A. (2002). The securitization of migration in western societies: Ambivalent discourses and policies. *Alternatives, 27*(1_suppl), 21–39.

first group is composed of arguments in which migration is cited as the cause of unemployment, of the crisis of the welfare state or of the devastation of an urban environment. The second group of arguments is made up of doubts raised by fears of loss of sovereignty and weakening of border controls, as well as an increase in crime. Along the identitarian axis, the arguments are related to threats to the national identity and demographic balance of the destination states of migration. Finally, anti-immigration and xenophobic attitudes are formulated around the fourth political axis in order to gain certain political advantages within the domestic political system. The electoral results of the far right show that anti-immigration attitudes can effectively mobilize voters. As we will see in the following pages, migration in Slovakia is securitized not only by the far right, but also by left-wing populist parties and even by a party that identifies itself as liberal.

For years, international migration has been a marginal topic of political discourse in Slovakia for several reasons. Compared to Western European countries, the total number of migrants with tolerated stays in Slovakia has been significantly lower. There were not enough pull factors in Slovakia to make it an attractive destination for migrants. Most migrants came from European Union countries or from culturally and linguistically related Slavic countries (especially Ukraine).[262] The number of migrants coming from religiously distinct countries was also low. The number of Muslims living in Slovakia was estimated in the literature at around 5,000 people; in the 2021 census, 3,862 persons claimed to be Muslims (in 2001 there were 1,212 Muslims and in 2011 – 1,934 Muslims). However, the total number of Muslims may be larger, because in the census, Muslims had to tick the "other" box next to religion and fill in the word "Islam" by hand. According to estimates by the Islamic Foundation in Slovakia,[263] some Muslims did not declare their religion due to distrust or indifference. This may be because Islam is not one of the state-recognized religions in Slovakia. In the past, some legislators from nationalist parties developed activities that complicated the registration of Islam as an official religion.

International migration as a topic of political discourse came to the attention of the Slovak political elite only in the context of the migration situation in

---

262   Štefančík, R., Némethová, I., & Seresová, T. (2021). Securitisation of migration in the language of Slovak far-right populism. *Migration Letters, 18*(6), 731–744.

263   Islamonline.sk (2020, January 20). Zverejnili údaje zo sčítania obyvateľov. K islamu sa prihlásilo 3862 moslimov. *Islamonline.sk.* https://www.islamonline.sk/2022/01/zverejnili-udaje-zo-scitania-obyvatelov-k-islamu-sa-prihlasilo-3862-moslimov

2015. Thousands of migrants from the Middle East and some African countries arrived on the European continent that year. Although the territory of Slovakia did not lie on the main migration routes, Slovak politicians were remarkably quick to take up the issue. The emergence of this topic among Slovak politicians could be explained first and foremost by the upcoming campaign for the parliamentary elections on 5 March 2016. In the election campaign, however, the pro-immigration and anti-immigration parties did not oppose each other. On the contrary, almost all of the relevant political parties expressed largely negative views on migrants. International migration, or rather the fear of migrants, became the central theme of the election campaign for several weeks. The debate was not repeated with similar intensity in the 2020 and 2023 election campaigns, although some politicians sporadically returned to the issue. As most political parties expressed negative attitudes towards migration, no special cleavage formed inside the party system dividing the parties of the two antagonistic camps.

There are several reasons for the negative attitude of the Slovak political elite towards migrants. It is not only during the election campaign, in which politicians find it easier to present anti-immigration attitudes. The negative stance of politicians was derived from the attitude of the public, which is predominantly negative towards migrants for two main reasons. The first is the relatively closed Slovak society which has its roots in the period of real socialism. Before 1989, not only emigration but also immigration was eliminated due to the closed borders. Czechoslovakia was mainly visited by nationals of friendly socialist states, albeit in limited numbers. Thanks to four decades of closed borders, Slovaks are a nation of old settlers who have no historical experience with the penetration of new cultural patterns of behaviour.[264] Majority of migrants today live in the capital or in larger cities, while the presence of migrants in smaller towns and villages was significantly lower until 2015. Communist propaganda also played a role in the negative attitude towards migrants. They were considered an important arch-enemy of the regime during the period of real socialism. Because they illegally crossed the borders of Czechoslovakia, migrants were also regarded to be criminals who, moreover, betrayed the ideals of the socialist society. The domestic regime may have considered migrants to be a danger to internal security since they were interrogated by the police or intelligence services of a Western European country (usually Germany or Austria) after crossing the border. Migrants thus embodied the characteristics of the class enemy. In the

---

264   Letavajová, S. (2018). *Zmiešané manželstvá (manželstvá s cudzincami ako sociokultúrny fenomén)*. Nitra: UKF v Nitre.

communist media they were presented as supporters of German Nazism, as American agents, or as clerical fascists.

Apart from the historical reasons for the prevailing negative attitude of Slovak society towards migrants, it is important to mention other reasons as well. One of them is the mostly negatively oriented coverage of the issue of migration, especially of Muslim migrants, by the Slovak media. It is also the absence of a concept of intercultural education of the young generation at primary and secondary schools. In Slovakia, young people have only limited opportunities to discuss international migration and the integration of immigrants during school lessons and to confront their own experiences with those of their classmates. The state does not promote the coexistence of people of different origins through the educational process, and the younger generation is then not sufficiently educated at schools to find an appropriate way to approach foreigners positively. This raises another problem, namely that Slovakia does not have a properly functioning concept of integration policy. Although there is a document formulating the basic principles of integration policy, it does not work well in practice. Slovakia has significant deficiencies in its integration policy, which is also evidenced by the conclusions of the analysis conducted by the international portal Migration Integration Policy Index (MIPEX). Which rated Slovakia's integration policy as below the average of the assessed countries (MIPEX 2020).[265]

5.1 Securitization of international migration as part of Slovak Populism

According to Hainsworth,[266] migration is an "issue par excellence" for populists. Extremely negative attitudes towards migration, including strong feelings of xenophobia, are among the "most characteristic topics of the far right."[267] In Slovakia, this issue was negatively articulated not only by representatives of the far right (ĽSNS, later Republika), but also by politicians from the democratic centre. A negative stance towards migrants was adopted by the left-wing Smer-SD party, as well as the liberal SaS party. As a rule, Slovak politicians constructed

---

265   MIPEX (2020). *Slovakia*. MIPEX. https://www.mipex.eu/slovakia
266   Hainsworth, P. (1992). *The extreme right in Europe and the USA*. New York: St Martin's Press, p. 7.
267   Lazaridis, G., & Tsagkroni, V. (2015). Securitisation of migration and far right populist othering in Scandinavian countries. In G. Lazaridis, & K. Wadia (Eds.), *The Securitisation of Migration in the EU Debates since 9/11*(pp. 207–236). London: Palgrave Macmillan.

four levels of threat: personal, cultural, economic and political, which roughly corresponds to the results of the analysis of Ceyhan and Tsoukal.[268]

(a) Migration as a threat to life or health

At the first level, migrants are presented as posing a threat to the life and health of the indigenous population. Slovak politicians have presented migrants either as potential criminals, even terrorists, or as carriers of various foreign diseases to Europe. They were supposed to arrive in Europe through green borders without any institution sufficiently verifying their identity. The populists promoted the idea that the migrants included some who are an immediate threat to the personal security (life, health) of the inhabitants of their countries of destination.

> SL → *Áno, povinné kvóty musíme odmietnuť. Pri existencii Islamského štátu, rastúcej* **náboženskej neznášanlivosti,** *akú zosobňujú* **islamskí radikáli,** *utečenci z Afriky a Ázie pre našich občanov predstavujú určité bezpečnostné riziko* (Ľubomír Galko).[269]
>
> SL → *Áno, rozumiem obavám z možnej* **infiltrácie vyslúžilých islamských bojovníkov.** *Rozumiem obavám z toho, že sa jednoducho väčšina z týchto ľudí* **nedokáže prispôsobiť** *životu v našich podmienkach, v našom svete* (Martin Fedor).[270]
>
> SL → *Som človek, ktorý ako premiér videl* **všelijaké hrôzy.** *Toto nie je hrôza, toto je* **nebezpečenstvo** (Robert Fico)[271]

The claims about criminal migrants or carriers of foreign diseases in the process of securitization has never been supported by Slovak politicians with relevant arguments. There are no statistics available in Slovakia to prove the above

---

268   Ceyhan, Tsoukala, 2002.

269   EL → Yes, we must reject mandatory quotas. With the existence of the Islamic State, the growing **religious intolerance** as personified by **Islamic radicals**, refugees from Africa and Asia poses a certain security risk to our citizens. Galko, Ľ. (2015, June 24). *Spoločná Česko-Slovenská Digitálna parlamentná knižnica, Archív.* Stenozáznam Parliament of the Slovak Republic. https://www.nrsr.sk/dl.

270   EL → Yes, I understand the concerns about the possible **infiltration of retired Islamist fighters**. I understand the fear that most of these people simply **cannot adapt to life** in our circumstances, in our world. Fedor, M. (2015, June 24). Spoločná Česko-Slovenská Digitálna parlamentná knižnica, Archív. Stenozáznam Parliament of the Slovak Republic. https://www.nrsr.sk/dl

271   EL → I am a man who has seen **all sorts of horrors** as a Prime Minister. This is not horror, this is **danger**. Tlačová agentúra Slovenskej republiky (2016, March 2). Toto nie je hrôza, toto je nebezpečenstvo, vyhlásil Fico po návšteve migrantov v Macedónsku. *Honline.sk.* https://hnonline.sk/slovensko/593159-toto-nie-je-hr-za-toto-je-nebezpecenstvo-vyhlasil-fico-po-navsteve-migrantov-v-macedonsku

statements. And that is why the favourite mode of argumentation of all populists comes to the forefront of the securitization strategy, i.e., "argument by analogy", which in practice means " referring to the analogy of a given case with other cases in the hope that these similarities will make it easier for the addressees to understand or to persuade them more effectively [...] the premises of the argument provide non-deductive support in favour of the truth of their conclusions, and this can often be very strong and reliable support."[272] Thus, politicians have based their intimidation rhetoric on well-known media cases from Western European countries. One of them, for example, was information about a case from New Year's Eve in Cologne, during which sexual assaults were allegedly committed by men of foreign origin.[273] By referring to such cases, although far beyond Slovakia's borders, migrants become a security risk even in the imagination of Slovak citizens. Ceyhan and Tsoukala[274] argue that emphasizing the criminal nature of illegal migration has "turned migrants without IDs into 'deviants' who must be kept under surveillance". As a result, many residents of the destination state of migration consider all migrants, regardless of their country of origin and the nature of their entry into the territory of the state, to be suspicious persons who need to be strictly monitored. Securitarian policy has thus come to be regarded as the principal way of countering irregular migration.

Representatives of the far right (from 2015 to 2020 it was mainly the People's Party Our Slovakia – ĽSNS) were exceptionally active in articulating personal threats. They often portrayed migrants as criminals aimed at physically threatening European (Slovak) women, sometimes even with racist connotations. Incidents from Western European countries, large European cities with segregated migrant communities, are often used as negative examples. Such arguments are generally not substantiated by statistics. Reference to a specific case is used as a generalizing characterization of migrants of a particular nationality or religion.

SL → Hovoril o *znásilňovaní bielych žien*, ktorého sa vo Švédsku dopúšťajú imigranti z Ázie a Afriky (ĽSNS, 2016).[275]

---

272 Zouhar, 2022, p. 121.
273 Tlačová agentúra Slovenskej republiky (2016, February 5). Z karnevalu v Kolíne nad Rýnom hlásia sexuálne útoky a znásilnenie. *Teraz.sk*, https://www.teraz.sk/zahrani cie/policia-v-koline-dostala-224-udani/180328-clanok.html
274 Ceyhan, Tsoukala 2002, p. 28.
275 EL → He spoke about **the rapes of white women** committed by immigrants from Asia and Africa in Sweden (ĽSNS 2016).

SL → *Problém nastáva až vtedy, keď sa cez otvorené hranice privalí invázia nelegálnych imigrantov, z ktorých mnohí neprichádzajú zo skutočnej núdze, ale prichádzajú si sem len zadarmo užívať,* **kradnúť, znásilňovať** *a* **vraždiť** (ĽSNS, 2018).[276]

SL → **Desiatky bielych žien sú znásilňované každý deň. Kriminalita závratne stúpa** *a* **gangy imigrantov** *sa medzi sebou v mestách strieľajú samopalmi. Západ a sever Európy je už* **stratený,** *nedovoľme, aby tak dopadlo aj Slovensko* (ĽSNS, 2018).[277]

SL → **Multikultúrne znásilňované Európanky,** *horiace policajné autá, či minarety namiesto kostolných veží, sú smutnou realitou západu v čoraz väčšej miere* (Marian Kotleba).[278]

(b) Migration as a cultural threat

The second level of threat is immediately related to the first. At this level, migrants are represented as a cultural threat or a factor threatening cultural or religious identity. This ethnopluralist approach is based on the idea that a nation is made up of one culture which needs to be protected from "foreign influence from the outside". Slovak politicians portray the inhabitants of Slovakia as a monocultural nation, as Christians, while the migrants threatening Slovak culture are supposed to come mainly from the Muslim world. At this level, migrants are portrayed as people whose cultural patterns of behaviour are incompatible with the culture of Slovaks.

SL → **Islam viacej mečom,** *kresťanstvo tak isto to robilo občas mečom, ale iným spôsobom, má to vo svojom poslaní, a v tomto narážajú a narážali stále na seba. A prečo to hovorím? Preto, že* **si nemyslím, že je dobré a sme schopní koexistovať** *tak, že istým spôsobom na pôde európskej rozsejeme, doslova rozsejeme semená, by som povedal, islamu* (Martin Fronc).[279]

---

276 EL → The problem only arises when an invasion of illegal immigrants rolls across the open borders, many of whom do not come here out of real need, but simply come here to enjoy themselves for free, **to steal, rape and murder** (ĽSNS 2018).

277 EL → **Dozens of white women are raped** every day. **Crime is skyrocketing** and **gangs of immigrants** are shooting each other with machine guns in cities. The West and the North of Europe **are already lost,** let's not lose Slovakia too (ĽSNS 2018).

278 EL → **Multicultural rapes of European women,** burning police cars, or minarets instead of church towers are a sad reality of the West still more and more. Kotleba, M. (2019). *Časopis Naše Slovensko.* ĽSNS. http://www.naseslovensko.net/casopis-nase-slovensko

279 EL → **Islam more by the sword,** Christianity also did it by the sword at times, but in a different way, this is in its mission, and they clash and have always clashed in this. And why am I saying it? Because **I don't think it is good and that we are capable of coexisting** in such a way that somehow on European soil we are sowing, literally sowing the seeds, I would say, of Islam. Fronc, M. (2015, June 24). *Spoločná Česko-Slovenská Digitálna parlamentná knižnica, Archív. Stenozáznam.* NRSR. https://www.nrsr.sk/dl

SL → *Je len na nás, či si necháme* **zdecimovať** *vlastnú krajinu. Či necháme moslimov postaviť si mešity na Slovensku. Či realitou zajtrajška budú zahalené ženy v burkách chodiace po slovenských mestách a dedinách* (Milan Mazurek).[280]

SL → *A je tu vidieť, aký je aj* **rozdiel medzi kresťanským a moslimským svetom** (Štefan Kuffa).[281]

SL → *Inými slovami* **Sorosov zahraničný agent** *na Slovensku financuje imigrantov, ktorí zaplavujú Európu a ktorí sú* **obrovskou hrozbou pre našu kresťanskú civilizáciu** (Rastislav Schlossár).[282]

The importance of culture is of great relevance to some Slovak voters as inhabitants of a small country that was founded only in 1993. Immediately after the systemic change in 1989, some politicians stressed the importance of cultural differences between the Czech nation and Slovaks as one of the arguments for the partition of Czechoslovakia. The second half of the 1990s was characterized by a sharp national conflict between the Slovak majority and the Hungarian minority. Nowadays, conflicting themes regularly emerge in the context of the so-called culture war, in which the progressive part of the population is pitted against the defenders of traditional values, based, among other things, on Christian tradition. It is these voters who are then prone to accept the argument that migrants can change the Christian nature of Slovak society.

In the literature, one can find the view that social Darwinist perspectives and a distinct, albeit modified, form of (modern) racism, in which extremists deliberately avoid using the lexeme race lie behind the expression cultural identity of a nation. This word usually has a negative connotation; therefore, it is frequently replaced by expressions such as culture, ethnicity, people, nation, or similar expressions. This approach is also commonly referred to as "raceless racism",[283] which abandons the lexeme "race" without making the

---

280 EL → It is entirely up to us whether we allow our own country **to be destroyed.** Whether we let Muslims build mosques in Slovakia. Whether the reality of tomorrow will be veiled women in burqas walking around Slovak towns and villages. Mazurek, M. (2015). *Časopis Naše Slovensko.* ĽSNS. http://www.naseslovensko.net/casopis-nase-slovensko

281 EL → And here you can see what **the difference is between the Christian and the Muslim world.** Kuffa, Š. (2015, June 24). *Spoločná Česko-Slovenská Digitálna parlamentná knižnica, Archív. Stenozáznam.* NRSR. https://www.nrsr.sk/dl

282 EL → In other words, **Soros's foreign agent** in Slovakia is financing immigrants who are flooding Europe and who are **a huge threat to our Christian civilization.** Schlossár, R. (2016, October 27). *Spoločná Česko-Slovenská Digitálna parlamentná knižnica, Archív. Stenozáznam.* NRRS. https://www.nrsr.sk/dl

283 Balibar, E., & Wallerstein, I. (1992). *Rasse Klasse Nation. Ambivalente Identitäten.* Berlin: Argument Verlag.

devaluation and exclusion of the other less forceful. Unlike "classical" racism, this approach, referred to as ethnopluralism, does not necessarily underline the superiority of the nation; however, most representatives do raise the demand for the dominant status of European nations. According to this approach, every nation should have an equal right and an equal claim to its national and cultural identity, but importantly, this right should be exercised in its own place of origin, not in the territory of another state. Corresponding to this idea, the proponents of this school of thought take a fundamentally negative approach to migration. Since immigrants are perceived as a threat to culture and national identity, ethnopluralists primarily point to its negative consequences.

(c) Migration as an economic threat

During the migration situation in 2015 and 2016, Slovak politicians often emphasized that migrants arriving to the European continent from Syria or North African countries were not real refugees, but economic migrants. The term "economic migrant" in particular has become synonymous with the economic dimension of the threat in Slovak political discourse. In the political discourse, there was no debate at all about the potential benefits of international migration for the domestic economy, for the pension system, or about its positive effects on the demographic situation. On the contrary, the economic migrant was presented by Slovak politicians as someone who should not have access to the Slovak labour market.

The economic dimension of the threat was expressed in two areas. The first area (the referent object under threat) was the labour market. Migrants are supposed to be a threat to Slovakia because they represent competition for the domestic labour force. As those who work without a work permit, migrants are a cheaper alternative for employers than domestic workers. Paradoxically, during the administrations of Smer, a party with strongly anti-immigration attitudes, the total number of foreigners with residence permits in Slovakia was growing.

More often discussed within this dimension of threat, however, is how migrants threaten the social systems of migration destination countries. By using the term "economic migrant", politicians create the image of a person whose aim is not to find a safe and, perhaps, economically more advantageous environment for his or her life. Many Slovak politicians use the term "economic migrant" to describe a person who is dependent on social assistance and unable to economically integrate into society.

SL → *Ľudia, ktorí vybudovali náš štát a platia dane nemajú z čoho žiť, ale štát ide dávať milióny eur na starostlivosť o imigrantov, ktorí preň neurobili vôbec nič!* (ĽSNS).[284]

The economic dimension of international migration was also underlined in the context of the alternative proposal of flexible solidarity. The essence of this proposal was that a Member State of the European Union which refused to accept migrants on its territory would pay a contribution of a certain nominal amount for each person. This proposal was met with mostly negative reactions from Slovak politicians in 2023, although the same politicians in 2015 and 2016 often proposed flexible solidarity as one of the ways Slovakia could contribute to the migration situation.

SL → *To nemyslíte vážne. My máme platiť za každého človeka 20.000 eur? Za sto ľudí to bude dva milióny eur. To je šialené* (Milan Uhrík).[285]

(d) Migration as a political threat

This dimension of threat is linked to state sovereignty as a referent object in the migration policy-making process. Since 2015, several Slovak politicians have held negative views on the development of a common European migration policy. Extremely negatively, and almost unanimously, they rejected Brussels' proposal that migrants should be redistributed according to a certain mechanism, so-called mandatory quotas, even to those states that are not the final destinations of the migrants. According to Slovak politicians, the state would lose (endanger) its sovereignty. Slovakia thus refused to place itself in a subordinate relationship to the decision-making centres of the European Union.

SL → *Povinné kvóty je našou povinnosťou odmietnuť aj preto, lebo je výlučne právomocou suverénnej Slovenskej republiky samostatne rozhodnúť,* **kto do nej môže a kto do nej nemôže prísť** *(Ľubomír Galko).*[286]

SL → *Odmietame princíp povinných kvót (Ľuboš Blaha).*[287]

---

284   EL → The people who built our country and pay taxes have nothing to live on, but the state goes on giving millions of euros to care for immigrants who have done nothing for it! ĽSNS (2016) Časopis Naše Slovensko. ĽSNS. http://www.nasesloven sko.net/casopis-nase-slovensko

285   EL → You can't be serious. Are we supposed to pay 20,000 euros for each person? For a hundred people, it will be two million euros. That's crazy. Uhrík, M. (2023). Facebook. https://www.facebook.com/ing.milan.uhrik

286   EL → It is our duty to reject mandatory quotas also because it is the sole competence of the sovereign Slovak Republic to decide independently **who can and who cannot enter its territory**. Galko, Ľ. (2015). *Spoločná Česko-Slovenská Digitálna parlamentná knižnica, Archív, Stenozáznam.* https://www.nrsr.sk/dl

287   EL → We reject the principle of mandatory quotas. Blaha, Ľ. (2016). *Spoločná Česko-Slovenská Digitálna parlamentná knižnica, Archív, Stenozáznam.* https://www.nrsr.sk/dl

5.2 Securitization of illegal crossing of national borders

Slovak politicians proposed increased levels of border control as the key solution to migration processes, especially at the external borders of the European Union. As Slovakia was not on the main migration routes in 2015 and 2016, the government supported the deployment of Slovak police officers to southern Hungary to help guard the border. Slovak politicians periodically presented the argument that better border control would discourage migrants from entering the country illegally, which would ultimately reduce the number of migrants or prevent migration.

SL → *Preto sme za dodržiavanie* **hraníc** *a zákonov. A potrebujeme* **kontrolovať to,** *čo vchádza a čo vychádza* (Miroslav Číž).[288]

SL → *Schengenská hranica má byť nejako chránená, tak má byť* **chránená všade** (Juraj Blanár).[289]

SL → *Takže to najdôležitejšie je* **zabezpečiť** *južnú* **hranicu silne a bezpečne** (Ľudovít Kaník).[290]

SL → *Naďalej budeme trvať na tom, že pokiaľ nedôjde k dôslednej ochrane vonkajších hraníc, tak sa* **neuchránime pred negatívnymi dôsledkami** *migračnej krízy* (Robert Fico).[291]

Reflections on the relationship between better border control and migration may not be realistic, because past experience shows that the barbed wire fences between Czechoslovakia and Austria or Germany did not prevent the emigration of Czechoslovak citizens. It was seen as just one of the many obstacles to be overcome on the road to freedom.

According to Malcolm Anderson,[292] arguments articulating the need to guard borders against external dangers have an important symbolic role. It defines the

---

288 EL → That is why we stand for the respect of **borders** and laws. And we need to **control** what comes in and what goes out. Číž, M. (2015). *Spoločná Česko-Slovenská Digitálna parlamentná knižnica, Archív, Stenozáznam.* https://www.nrsr.sk/dl

289 EL → The Schengen border should be protected somehow, so it should be **protected everywhere.** Blanár, J. (2015). *Spoločná Česko-Slovenská Digitálna parlamentná knižnica, Archív, Stenozáznam.* https://www.nrsr.sk/dl

290 EL → So the most important thing is **to secure** the southern border **strongly and safely.** Kaník, Ľ. (2015). *Spoločná Česko-Slovenská Digitálna parlamentná knižnica, Archív, Stenozáznam.* https://www.nrsr.sk/dl

291 EL → We will keep insisting that we **will not be able to protect ourselves from the negative consequences** of the migrant crisis unless the external borders are rigorously protected. Fico, R. (2016). *Predseda vlády Robert Fico a minister vnútra Robert Kaliňák navštívili macedónsko – grécku hranicu.* Úrad vlády SR. https://www.vlada.gov.sk/predseda-vlady-robert-fico-a-minister-vnutra-robert-kalinak-navstiv ili-macedonsko-%E2%80%93-grecku-hranicu

292 Anderson, M. (1996). *Frontiers, territory and state formation in the modern world.* Cambridge: Polity Press.

territory of a sovereign state which should remain inviolable. Each state has set conditions under which it is possible to enter its territory. Migrants are presented as a danger because many of them cross the borders of a sovereign state illegally. Thus, from the very beginning of their stay in the country, irregular migrants are perceived as criminals in the eyes of voters with radical mindsets. Such prejudice, reinforced by securitizing political statements, subsequently hinders the creation of a positive image of migrants.

5.3 Metaphor in migration discourse

Political communication has always been saturated with metaphors. In the context of metaphor research, there is a famous statement by Seth Thompson that "politics without metaphors is like a fish without water. A fish needs water to be a fish. And people need metaphors to do politics and reason about it."[293] Charlotte Taylor,[294] who based on her research of the English press since the late 18th century, has developed six basic categories of metaphors used in the context of migration:

- *Water or liquid:* Water-related expressions have a negative effect on people because they are associated with circumstances such as chaos, instability and danger (*migratory wave, migratory flows, flood of migrants*).
- *Migrants as objects* or *commodities*: Given that Taylor (2021) analysed the British press from the late 18th century onwards, these metaphors appeared mainly in the context of the human or slave trade. Later, they can be identified in the context of the discussion on cheap labour from abroad.
- *Terms from the animal world (often animals that cause harm to humans)*: In her analysis, Taylor often identified terms such as *parasites* or *pests*, *vermin*. The connotations evoked by these terms are extremely negative.
- *Migrants as an enemy* or *aggressor*: Another negative approach to migrants. Taylor stresses that this category of metaphors does not dehumanize migrants, but it induces a sense of threat.
- *Migrants as guests*: Taylor identifies the unequal relationship between the native population and those arriving in the host community. The metaphor of guest has been conventionalized as guest (invited) worker, especially in the

---

293   Thompson, S. (1996). Politics without metaphors is like a fish without water. In J. S. Mio, & A. N. Katz (Eds), *Metaphor: Implications and applications* (pp. 185–201). Mahwah, NJ: Lawrence Erlbaum Associates.
294   Taylor, Ch. (2021). Metaphors of migration over time. *Discourse & Society, 32*(4), 463–481.

German postwar context (Taylor, 2021), when invited economic migrants (*Gastarbeiter*) helped to solve the labour shortage during the period of economic growth.

- *Metaphor of a load or burden*: this metaphor is mainly used in an economic context, where migrants are perceived as having a negative impact on the domestic economy.

Similar categories of metaphors can be encountered in the contemporary Slovak migration discourse. Several of the negative metaphors securitize the topic of migration because they deliberately evoke a sense of threat, which results in the creation of a negative attitude towards migrants.

(a) Water metaphor

This metaphor is exceptionally frequent in Slovak migration discourse, which in itself does not necessarily imply a sense of threat. It is even frequent in professional and scientific language. Scientists in Slovakia usually use the term *"migration wave of 2015 and 2016"* without intending to evoke negative feelings in the recipients of the given information (these are so-called dead or lexicalized metaphors). Even the phrase *"migration crisis"* is used extremely frequently in scholarly discourse, although it was not a crisis of migration, but rather a crisis of European migration policy. This category of metaphor assumes a different character when it is used with the deliberate purpose of evoking a negative attitude towards migration processes in the domestic audience:

SL → *Vlna migrácie sa sem bude **valiť** ďalej* (Ľudovít Kaník).[295]
SL → *Aby sme Vám mohli ukázať pravú tvár tejto **katastrofy**, tak sme navštívili niekoľko európskych krajín najviac **postihnutých imigračnou vlnou*** (Milan Uhrík).[296]

In this context, migration is represented as a catastrophe. The metaphor of water carries a negative connotation; the destination states of migration are supposed to be afflicted ("flooded") by migration. This term conveys the impression that migration is a phenomenon with explicitly negative consequences for the security of the inhabitants of the state of destination. In addition to the word

---

295 EL → The wave of migration will continue **rolling in**. Kaník, Ľ. (2015). *Spoločná Česko-Slovenská Digitálna parlamentná knižnica, Archív, Stenozáznam.* https://www.nrsr.sk/dl

296 EL → To show you the true face of this **catastrophe**, we visited several European countries most **affected by the immigration wave**. Uhrík, M. (2023). Facebook. https://www.facebook.com/ing.milan.uhrik

wave, terms such as *tide, inflow,* and *flood*, or the verb *to overflow*, also appear in the migration discourse. In the following cases it is necessary to distinguish the context in which they are employed. Stopping the *flow* of migrants appears to be a political objective with no apparent intention of stirring up negative emotions. However, the context in which the author connects the migration *wave* with terrorist and sexual attacks or the arrival of "dangerous people" is different:

> SL → *Prílev migrantov môže byť spojený aj s **prítokom** nebezpečných ľudí* (Robert Fico).[297]
> SL → *Nevyhnutnosťou je zastaviť **tok migrantov*** (Robert Kaliňák).[298]
> SL → ***Migračná vlna**, ktorá je nekontrolovaná a neriadená, má súvis s teroristickými i sexuálnymi útokmi. Politici v europarlamente nás zradili a **zaplavujú** Európu miliónmi migrantov* (ĽSNS).[299]

(b) Migrants as objects or commodities

Taylor (2021) associates this category of metaphor with trafficking in people as slaves, or with the context of inviting foreigners as cheap labour. In the Slovak political discourse this category of metaphor is not very frequent. Slovakia has no experience with human trafficking, and politicians do not speak openly about solving the workforce shortage or the demographic crisis through a regulated immigration policy. Instead, it appears in connection with the criticism of the unregulated migration processes of 2015 and 2016:

> *Iná vláda by na Slovensko **navozila** tisícky migrantov* (Robert Fico).[300]

(c) Migrants as animals

The animal metaphor was a regular part of the vocabulary of the far-right (ĽSNS, currently Republika) when they first entered parliament in 2016. This metaphor

---

297 EL → The influx of migrants may also be accompanied by an **influx** of dangerous people. Fico, R. (2015). *Fico: Prílev migrantov môže byť spojený aj s prítokom nebezpečných ľudí.* Úrad vlády SR. https://www.vlada.gov.sk/fico-prilev-migrantov-moze-byt-spojeny-aj-s-pritokom-nebezpecnych-ludi

298 EL → It is necessary to stop **the flow of migrants**. Kaliňák, R. (2016). *Smer-SD Website*. https://stwebsmer.strana-smer.sk

299 EL → **The migration wave**, which is uncontrolled and unregulated, is linked to both terrorist and sexual attacks. Politicians in the European Parliament have betrayed us and **are flooding** Europe with millions of migrants. ĽSNS (2019). *ĽSNS Website*. http://www.naseslovensko.net

300 EL → A different government **would have brought** thousands of migrants to Slovakia. Fico, 2016.

was used mainly in the context of a critical attitude towards the domestic Roma minority. The term *parasites* was a natural part of their vocabulary before the general election. Upon their entry into parliament in 2016 and after the Attorney General's attempts to ban the activities of ĽSNS, they adjusted their vocabulary and stopped using some terms. As a result, the animal metaphors have to be sought in their earlier activities, especially in the period before they entered parliament. However, the animal metaphor continues to be used by other political actors; even the current Speaker of Parliament creates a sense of threat referring to the migrant tent city in this way:

SL → *Tu sa migranti potulujú po poliach, ako také **myši** tam* pobehujú (Boris Kollár).[301]

(d) Migrants as enemies

Thinking about politics in terms of friend vs enemy is perhaps as old as politics itself. Similar perceptions of political opponents can be identified in Slovak political discourse. A considerable degree of polarization of Slovak society has been present since the systemic change in 1989, or since the beginning of the building of a competitive party system. Political parties treat each other as enemies; cooperation between some political parties is ruled out because of personal animosities or ideological divisions. Similarly polarized is the perception of elements that do not fit into the traditional understanding of the nation. In the past, for many far-right parties, members of the Hungarian minority or Hungary as a state were presented as enemies of the nation; today, members of allochthonous minorities, especially migrants from culturally different regions, are considered enemies of the nation. In particular, Muslims and economic migrants are considered to be enemies that threaten the security of the domestic population:

*V situácii, keď je celá Európa ohrozovaná **votrelcami** z Afriky či Ázie, keď jej hrozí islamizácia a rozvrat našej viery, štátov, kultúry a tradícií* (ĽSNS, 2015).[302]
*Sú to **násilní votrelci**, pred ktorými sa Európa musí brániť* (Richard Sulík).[303]

---

301   EL → Here migrants run around the fields like **mice** (Boris Kollár, 2022).

302   EL → In a situation when the whole of Europe is threatened by **intruders** from Africa or Asia, when it is threatened by Islamization and the subversion of our faith, states, culture, and traditions. Kollár, B. (2022, November 9). *Boris Kollár straší nelegálnymi migrantmi. Denník N.* https://dennikn.sk/minuta/3099412

303   EL → They are **violent intruders** and Europe must defend itself against them. Sulík, R. (2018). *Spoločná Česko-Slovenská Digitálna parlamentná knižnica, Archív, Stenozáznam.* https://www.nrsr.sk/dl

*Akoby nestačilo to, že tu máme cigánsky problém, už sa na nás valia **hordy** moslimských imigrantov* (ĽSNS, 2016).[304]

(e) Migrants as guests

The debate about inviting migrants, mostly as cheap labour, dominated in the context of rapid economic growth in the post-war period of the second half of the 20th century. Although Slovak government officials made frequent anti-immigration statements in 2015 and 2016, the total number of foreigners with residence permits in Slovakia was gradually increasing. On one hand, the Slovak government presented a negative attitude towards migrants; on the other hand, it created conditions for further employing foreign workers. However, they did not openly discuss this phenomenon, which is commonly referred to as *gap hypothesis* in political science literature. Inviting migrants was associated with negative connotations:

SL → *Napriek tomu sem EÚ **pozýva** ďalších imigrantov* (ĽSNS).[305]

(f) Migrants as a load or (economic) burden

When Slovak politicians talk about migration as a burden, they usually mean an economic burden. It can take two forms: (1) migrants as competition in the labour market or (2) migrants as a burden to the social system (expenditures on housing, social assistance and the placement of migrant children in pre-school institutions). Migration is thus perceived as a phenomenon that imposes various forms of burdens on home countries, while the benefits of migration are not discussed at all.

SL → *Mnohé tie krajiny, ktoré nesú tú zodpovednosť, tak to **bremeno** chcú preniesť možno práve na tie krajiny, ktoré sme sa stali čerstvými alebo sme stále novými členmi Európskej únie … Ja za kvóty nie som* (Štefan Kuffa).[306]
SL → *Moslimskí … páchajú mnohé zločiny a sú **ohromnou záťažou** pre pôvodných obyvateľov* (ĽSNS, 2018).[307]

---

304   EL → As if it is not enough that we have a gypsy problem here, **hordes** of Muslim immigrants are already pouring in. ĽSNS, 2016.

305   EL → Nevertheless, the EU **is inviting** more immigrants here. ĽSNS, 2016.

306   EL → Many of those countries that bear the responsibility want to shift the **burden** perhaps to those countries that have just become or are still new members of the European Union … I am not in favour of quotas. Kuffa, Š. (2015). *Spoločná Česko-Slovenská Digitálna parlamentná knižnica, Archív, Stenozáznam.* https://www.nrsr.sk/dl

307   EL → Muslim … commit many crimes and are **a huge burden** for the native population. ĽSNS, 2018.

(g) War metaphor

Although Taylor (2021) does not talk about the war metaphor, in the context of anti-migration measures, politicians often use terms from the military lexicon. The war metaphor is a natural component of the politicians' language, not only across countries, but across time periods as well. For some politicians of the past and present, politics was and still is associated with the context of war. Whether it was an open military conflict using conventional weapons, or tensions between states or blocs of states but without an open military confrontation, such as during the Cold War, or in the context of a trade war, or a so-called hybrid war, or when it came to actions in the war against terrorism, politicians and journalists reporting on political events did not shy away from the term war. On the contrary, they have become a common and frequent means of expression. War metaphors come to the fore at critical moments, such as during the migration situation in 2015 and 2016, and to underline the importance of the measures taken, or when political activities are under greater public scrutiny, such as during election campaigns. Apart from the cases mentioned above, expressions connoting war will appear especially in the political vocabulary of those actors whose politics display a higher degree of verbal aggression. Specifically, they will be representatives of political extremism, irrespective of whether it is left-wing or right-wing extremism.

> SL → Ľudová strana Naše Slovensko bude vždy **bojovať** za to, aby Slovensko neprijalo ani jedného jediného imigranta! (Milan Mazurek, 2015).[308]
> SL → Násilní Afričania, Turci a Aziati úplne **obsadili** mnohé mestá (ĽSNS).[309]
> SL → Imigranti **obsadzujú** Európu (Stratená Európa).[310]

Our reflections are confirmed by the observations of Slovak experts who state that "extremely emotionally-coloured linguistic means are used to mark the arrival of immigrants, media images manipulate group identity, strictly distinguishing between individuals and groups on the basis of cultural distinctiveness, emphasizing and clearly defining polarity: "we/us" ("our", "domestic") and "they/ them" ("foreign", "different"). Negative feelings about the arrival of immigrants

---

308 EL → The People's Party Our Slovakia will always **fight for** Slovakia not to accept even one single immigrant! Mazurek, 2015.

309 EL → Violent Africans, Turks and Asians have completely **occupied** many cities. ĽSNS, 2018.

310 EL → Immigrants **are taking over** Europe. Stretená Európa (2019). *Imigranti obsadzujú Európu.* http://www.stratenaeuropa.sk/?fbclid=IwAR2xoaX-uYaEPfa qkm-VUc¬0t¬VS8id8ph7NnQiyyKmH8aj8iDqm6-22EPHUNI

are fuelled by the use of metaphors that evoke fear, threats, and the overpowering of our culture."[311]

5.4 From securitization to the attempts at the desecuritization of migration processes

As mentioned above, the topic of international migration entered the Slovak political discourse only in the context of the migration processes of 2015 and 2016. Politicians have grasped the issue in an overly negative way, which has resulted, among other things, in a shift in the meaning of some words associated with the issue. First of all, the meaning of the word *migrant* or *migration* has shifted. Before 2015, the term was neutral; in the post-2015 discourse, it has taken on a particularly negative meaning, despite the fact that Slovakia was neither a destination nor a transit country for migrants who were looking for a new home in European countries in 2015 and 2016.

A different situation occurred in February 2022 after the Russian military invasion of Ukraine. From the very first day, Slovakia had to deal with issues related to the mass arrival of the inhabitants of the neighbouring country. Many of them were heading further to other countries, but several tens of thousands remained in Slovakia (as of 10 July 2023, 104,251 foreigners with the purpose of seeking temporary refuge were registered).

The war in Ukraine was perceived differently by the Slovak population than the conflicts that resulted in migration processes in 2015 and 2016. This war was fought in the country of Slovakia's immediate neighbour, and the fleeing citizens were at the border practically on the same day as the Russian assault began. In response to the Ukrainian refugees, a degree of solidarity of the Slovak population was revealed. Slovaks spontaneously went to the Slovak-Ukrainian border to help Ukrainian refugees, and the extent of assistance from Slovak citizens, NGOs, private companies, and local government representatives surpassed that of the state authorities.

The positive attitude of the Slovak population towards Ukrainian migrants was influenced by three factors. The first was the immediate shock of the Russian military invasion. In spite of numerous reports of the movements of the Russian army in the immediate vicinity of the Ukrainian border, few foresaw an open act of military aggression. The second factor was the cultural affinity of the

---

311   Letavajová, S., Chlebcová Hečková A., Krno S., & Bošelová M. (2020). *Novodobé migrácie vo verejnej, mediálnej a politickej diskusii*. Nitra. Filozofická fakulta Univerzita Konštantína Filozofa v Nitre, p. 157.

inhabitants of Slovakia and Ukraine. Both nations belong to the group of Slavic peoples with related languages, cultural and religious traditions. They even share a similar past with the authoritarian regime of communist parties. Finally, the third factor was as important as the first two, namely the demographic composition of the incoming war refugees. While in 2015 and 2016, populists claimed that the migrants were predominantly men, and that they were mainly economic migrants and not refugees, in the case of Ukrainian refugees, women and children prevailed, and the reason for their arrival on the territory of Slovakia was unambiguous.

A different attitude of the Slovak public towards Ukrainian refugees could also be observed on the linguistic level. First of all, it was about the expressions used to refer to the refugees. Ukrainian refugees were referred to by the word "departees", a term with no direct connotation to migration processes, migrants or asylum seekers. That word was used both by official authorities (foreign police, migration office, statistical bureau) and the media, and became part of the political vocabulary. The Bureau of Border and Foreign Police kept special statistics on foreigners and departees. It is through the use of terms referring to Ukrainian war refugees that we can illustrate how the state seeks to eliminate negative stereotypical views of a particular group of migrants. At the same time, many Ukrainians have settled in Slovakia since 24 February 2022, found jobs and gradually integrated into Slovak society, with no concrete vision of their eventual return to their country of origin.

Hence, if we talk about securitization in our publication, we should not forget about desecuritization either. Wæver[312] introduces three ways to achieve desecuritization. In the first place, we should stop talking about a certain topic as a security issue. This could be seen, for example, in the migration discourse after the 2016 elections, when politicians marginalized the issue of international migration again. During the period of the governments of Robert Fico as the main critic of the European migration policy, the number of migrants in Slovakia was even gradually increasing. The trouble with this condition is that it only exists for a short period of time. As a rule, during election campaigns, migration is perceived as a problem again. Politicians use the articulation of fears of migrants, of the other, as a way of mobilizing voters, regardless of whether these

---

312 Wæver, O. (2000). The EU as a security actor: Reflections from a pessimistic constructivist on post-sovereign security orders. In M. Kelstrup, & M. Williams (Eds), *International Relations Theory and the Politics of European Integration: Power, Security, and Community* (pp. 250–294). London: Routledge.

fears are real or merely fictitious. The second way to achieve desecuritization is to maintain reactions that do not create "security dilemmas and other vicious spirals". Finally, the third way is to return to "normal politics". In the case of Slovak public discourse about war refugees from Ukraine, we have witnessed the process of desecuritization through speech acts. If we analyse speech acts that induce a sense of threat when researching securitization, we should do the same for the process of desecuritization, asking what expressive means political actors use to make an aspect that is usually perceived as a security threat into an aspect with no direct link to the issue of security. This is exactly what we have seen in the case of the Slovak discourse on refugees from Ukraine. Opinion leaders (with the exception of some populist parties) did not use the common linguistic terms *migrant* or *refugee*, which are common in migration research, to refer to migrants from Ukraine, as was typical of the migration discourse in 2015–2016. These very terms, originally neutral, have become synonymous with danger for many inhabitants through the continuous process of securitization. They have become expressions with predominantly negative connotations. However, this time Slovak opinion makers did the opposite and chose terms that were not associated with a threat to the security of the domestic population to describe the war refugees. Military aid to Ukraine (defence systems, fighter jets), though, has been presented as a possible threat to our economic prosperity, especially by the opposition parties. Nevertheless, migrants from Ukraine, precisely because of the language used, have not created a deeper sense of threat in the public. From this we can conclude that the use of specific expressions can also have a desecuritizing effect.

Although some institutions and opinion makers have referred to the war refugees from Ukraine by different terms than the migrants of 2015 and 2016, the tendency to securitize the issue of migration from Ukraine in political discourse has arisen. The involved politicians were mainly from far-left and far-right parties. In particular, those politicians drew attention to the criminal offences of some Ukrainian citizens, to competition on the labour market within certain sectors of the national economy, or to the refugees as a burden to the domestic social system. Given the proximity of the countries, the cultural dimension of the threat was absent. These attitudes demonstrate that securitization of migration for certain political parties is a solid part of their communication strategy. Emphasizing different dimensions of a threat (personal, economic, political or cultural) will depend on which country the migrants come from.

VI. Conclusion

In the process of analysing the Slovak public discourse on security over the past ten years (manifested mainly in the media and on social networks), we focused on the specificity of the language used to evoke a sense of threat and the associated negative (even protesting) emotions in the recipient (potential voter). Methodologically, we drew on the innovative premises of the Copenhagen School's securitization theory, which allowed us to conceptualize the induction of a sense of threat and the necessity to approach security measures as a discursive practice and to perceive the act of securitization as a speech act that creates new meanings and is capable of inciting certain social dynamics. In spite of our analysis of the potential benefits of interdisciplinary (politolinguistic) research on the processes of securitization in the first chapter, we must emphasize that this analysis was not of a political science nature (it did not evaluate the relevance of the content of the statements nor did it examine which statements are disinformation, deliberate lies, deliberate distortions of facts or conspiracy theories). The focus of the analysis was on the linguistic (mainly lexical) level of the utterances of politicians, by which we intended to show which linguistic means increase the manipulative effect of speech acts and thus facilitate the process of securitization.

The principal aim of our research was to analyse the securitizing speech acts produced by prominent actors of Slovak public discourse who have presented fabricated social threats to a broad audience in order to achieve their political goals. Unlike the Copenhagen School scholars who focus on the "when, how and on the basis of whose activity a topic becomes a security threat"[313] in their analysis of security discourse, we analysed "textual character as a defining criterion of security, on the specific rhetorical structures of discursive practice."[314] Our research did not examine whether something is legitimately or illegitimately articulated as a security threat; we investigated how alleged threats are verbalized, which linguistic devices the authors of threat articulations use most frequently in presenting them, and the persuasive effects of their use.

In the process of exploration (which included research using the Sketch Engine corpus manager), we arrived at the following conclusions:

---

313   Buzan, Wæver, & De Wilde, 1998.
314   Buzan, Wæver, & De Wilde, 1998.

- Numerous Slovak actors of securitization (mostly representatives of nationalist ideologies, right-wing and left-wing radicals, proponents of Euroscepticism, extremism, political and cultural Russophilia), as the main threatened entities (reference objects), focus on the economic security of Slovakia, democracy, social security of Slovaks, food security, rule of law, "traditional" family values, traditional Christian values, "distinctive culture" and traditions, Slovak cultural identity and, more broadly, the so-called "historical Slavic unity", sovereignty and territorial integrity of the Slovak Republic, public health and safety of citizens, freedom of the media and freedom of expression, peace, human and civil dignity.

Who do they believe are the greatest threats to these entities? First and foremost, it is liberals, sun worshippers, pro-European parties and movements, NGOs, the EU/Brussels/"European bureaucracy", NATO, George Soros, President Čaputová, coalition parties, the USA, the "Zelensky regime" and migrants. We believe that the continuous articulation of events related to the war in Ukraine as hypertrophied threats is one of key reasons for the rise of Euroscepticism, isolationist tendencies and extremist sentiments in Slovak society.

- The name of George Soros is repeated like a mantra in the securitization discourse, and as a concept it reaches an almost unlimited semantic range and an extraordinary variability of associations. As a symbolic anthroponym and pejorative figure of speech, the use of Soros's name is crucial for the entire Slovak securitization discourse (of a conspiratorial, radical, populist orientation), and it is here that the appellativization of his name (when a proper name becomes a common noun) can be stated to have been completed in the Slovak linguistic image of the world. Uttering the name of Soros becomes an "unquestionable" argument in the fight of political populists with liberals, NGOs, NATO, President Čaputová and other "anti-Slovak elements".
- The evocation of a sense of threat need not be of a "straightforward" explicit nature (the words safety, threat, danger do not have to be spoken), but expressive, emotionally-coloured terms, expressive clichéd phrases, conflictogenic metaphors, hyperboles, phrasemes used in securitizing speech acts as well as expressions with strong negative connotations, substandard lexis (sociolects, jargonisms, argot, vulgarisms), sophisticated (and simplified) historical allusions, publicisms and impressive linguoculturalisms are able to induce a sense of danger quickly, reliably and permanently by acting on the sphere of emotions. Particularly impressive are the hyperbolic means of expression and negativizing adjectives (*vagabond minister, traitorous treaty with the USA, gigantic debt, godless sacrilege, monstrous spectacle*), and stigmatizing

and dehumanizing expressions of a metaphorical nature (*slimy snakes, media vultures*). As can be seen from the example of the 2023 pre-election securitization processes, they resonate with certain audiences (translated into pre-election preferences). Based on our research, we can conclude that the increasing "colloquiality" and speech aggression of texts with manipulative securitizing intent is a significant trend in Internet-mediated communication.

– The dichotomous perception of reality in the sense of WE/US and THEY/ THEM, THE OTHERS, or THE STRANGERS is also significant. In the spirit of the traditional speech strategy of populists ONE OF YOU – TO MY FOLKS (I think like you – I speak like you, your linguistic means are also mine), Slovak securitization actors fulfil the "criterion of intelligibility" to the maximum extent possible. Their speech acts are sophisticated in the sense of selecting linguistic means as close as possible to the linguistic traditions and linguistic (stylistically predominantly colloquial) culture of their target audience (they include numerous expressive colloquial phrases *to play it like a loudmouth, to fall into a sewer, to break through the bottom, as if out of his senses, to throw oneself a noose, not to do shit,* invective lexis, a number of ungrammatical, slang, taboo and substandard words, as well as conspicuous emotional-expressive lexical stylemes).

– Securitizing speech acts on social networks are highly redundant in nature, but an analysis of comments made by followers suggests that they simply do not pay attention and never criticize. From a linguistic point of view, the constant repetition can also be seen as the deliberate creation of stylistic figures (anaphora, epiphora, epizeuxis, anadiplosis, parallelism, etc.), but in that case, we should see the status texts of securitization actors as artistic. However, the extraordinary speed of production of the analysed texts (at least one per day, but often several hours apart) does not allow them to go beyond the colloquial style (in written form), which is, after all, typical of most Facebook statuses.

– Slovak securitization discourse, which regards various social phenomena as potential threats to diverse referent objects, results, among other things, in a shift in meanings (re-semantization) of individual denominations that have traditionally been used to refer to them. For example, the meaning of the originally neutral term "migrant" has become negative in the context of the extremely negatively-charged securitization debate fuelled by SMER party representatives before the Slovak parliamentary elections of 2016 and 2023, and is currently associated with "security threat", "threat to the cultural identity of Slovaks", "threat to the economic prosperity of Slovaks", etc. Our research indicates that even units that previously seemed semantically neutral (liberalism, multiculturalism, NGOs, progressivism) are subject to significant resemanticization in the process of securitization, and expressions of an oxymoronic nature (such as liberal fascism, "sun-worshipping" extremist) are becoming more frequent. Moreover, in the process of securitization, the established dominant ideologemes or more narrowly perceived politemes of public discourse (power, state, politics, ideology, government, parliament, political party) acquire new connotations and thus a new axiological dimension, which may lead to a change in the nature of political discourse and deepen the crisis of values that is currently manifesting itself in various spheres of social life.

– Today, a significant securitization vector in Slovakia is directed towards the articulation of threats to physiological needs, security, social security, but also social acceptance, belonging, recognition and respect. We have also observed a new discursive strategy in recent years (mostly by right-wing extremists and left-wing populists) that could be described as the securitization of the "human dignity" of their target audience (potential voter base) which is constantly being threatened by government representatives, political figures, official media and representatives of liberal, pro-European movements, who, according to the aforementioned securitization actors, continuously insult and underestimate the so-called "common people". Through these unsubstantiated "assaults" on the "common people", securitization actors make the general public feel that their social acceptance, dignity, recognition, and respect are threatened, which proves to be a productive discursive strategy (with a strong persuasive effect).

– The comparative corpus research of texts published in the online version of *Denník N* from 2015 to 2022 (a liberal newspaper) and texts (including blogs) published in the *Hlavné správy* online periodical from 2013 to 2022 (we coded it as an anti-liberal periodical and a popular conspiracy and disinformation website) revealed a significant prevalence of metaphors of a conflictual nature (*Satan* metaphor, zoomorphic metaphors *monkey, hyena, shark, octopus*, and criminal metaphors *mafia* and *crime*) in the *Hlavné správy* online periodical.

– The analysis of securitizing speech acts in social networks (Facebook, Telegram) of successful representatives of Slovak left-wing populism, Robert Fico, the chairman of the opposition (2020–2023) party SMER, and its vice-chairman Ľuboš Blaha pointed to their distinct metaphorical nature. In the process of securitization, the actors in question tend to turn to the usual or even stereotypical images (most often referring to notorious facts of history). It is also possible to speak of a considerable instrumentalization of history (in favour of the author's intentions, especially in the case of events and names connected with the glorified "big Russian brother" and the idea of Slavic mutuality), as well as the construction of extremely conflictogenic metaphorical concepts, while in both cases the most frequently used conceptual scheme (frame) is clearly *fascism* (which is represented by a number of thematically correlated slots such as *Gestapo, Hitler, Goebbels, concentration camps, Auschwitz*). The consistent instrumentalization of history accompanied by a reinterpretation of ideologies, for example, the concept of *fascism*, precisely defined from the viewpoint of political science (which in the discourse of Blaha and Fico semantically covers everything that does not suit them personally and their political intentions and which is endlessly repeated in totally different contexts from status to status) leads to a slow but certain emptying of its original meaning, de-ideologization and, consequently, to value disorientation in terms of the historical and cultural memory of the young generation of Slovaks.

The qualitative and quantitative analysis of securitizing discourse metaphors of the aforementioned actors shows an absolute predominance of conflictogenic metaphors, which indicates their efforts to enhance the manipulative effect of speech acts and to intensify social tensions. These are primarily metaphorical models with conceptual vectors of aggression (military and criminal metaphors), metaphors of deviation from the natural course of things (morbial metaphors), metaphors pointing to the improbability of events (theatrical metaphors), to material calculativeness (financial metaphors), zoomorphic dehumanizing metaphors (pig, dog, donkey), anthropomorphic metaphors (mostly physiological: dirty hands, empty head, break your back, clean the brain), beastly metaphors (Satan, devil, fiend) and destructive metaphors (natural cataclysms, catastrophes, decay, disintegration, devastation). The most frequent in the discourse of Fico and Blaha turned out to be expressive war metaphors, frightening morbial metaphors (*death, cancer, insane asylum, suicide, mental illness*) theatrical metaphors (*circus, comedy, farce*) financial metaphors (*business deals for the US, bargains*) and zoomorphic metaphors (*rams, rats, barking, herd, snakes*).

The monitored securitization process of Ľuboš Blaha and Robert Fico on social networks can be evaluated as successful, since at the end of August 2022 the representatives of Smer-SD submitted over 406,039 signatures of citizens calling for a referendum on the dissolution of the government and changes to the Constitution of the Slovak Republic, as a result of which the President announced a referendum on pre-term elections. Almost half a million people believed the threats articulated by the influential actors of securitization.

We argue that research similar to ours (based on a textual understanding of securitization as a socially productive speech act that legitimates politicians to take urgent action to neutralize "existential threats") has the potential not only to explain how a sense of threat is created in referent objects through a speech act, and (as a secondary yet important implication) it can help elucidate the inner mechanisms of the accelerating (dis)information war. In this context, among other things, the urgent question of the responsibility of the securitizing actor for the choice of linguistic means and meanings of speech acts arises, because the conflictogenic metaphors of the lexical domain of *hate speech* inevitably direct public discourse towards an increase in aggression. Tensions in society are rising and this suits all political actors, because the shortest and surest route to increase the number of adherents is securitization, since presenting dangers to a certain community immediately ties it together and becomes the most convenient form of ideological consolidation.

Corpus resources

Blaha, Ľ. (2016). *Spoločná Česko-Slovenská Digitálna parlamentná knižnica, Archív, Stenozáznam.* https://www.nrsr.sk/dl

Blaha, Ľ. (2021). Facebook. https://www.facebook.com/LBlaha

Blaha, Ľ. (2023, April). Telegram. https://t.me/s/LubosBlahaSmer

Blanár, J. (2015). *Spoločná Česko-Slovenská Digitálna parlamentná knižnica, Archív, Stenozáznam.* https://www.nrsr.sk/dl

Číž, M. (2015). *Spoločná Česko-Slovenská Digitálna parlamentná knižnica, Archív, Stenozáznam.* https://www.nrsr.sk/dl

Fedor, M. (2015, June 24). *Spoločná Česko-Slovenská Digitálna parlamentná knižnica, Archív. Stenozáznam* https://www.nrsr.sk/dl

Fico, R. (2015). *Fico: Prílev migrantov môže byť spojený aj s prítokom nebezpečných ľudí.* Úrad vlády SR. https://www.vlada.gov.sk/fico-prilev-migrantov-moze-byt-spojeny-aj-s-pritokom-nebezpecnych-ludi

Fico, R. (2016). *Predseda vlády Robert Fico a minister vnútra Robert Kaliňák navštívili macedónsko – grécku hranicu.* Úrad vlády SR. https://www.vlada.gov.sk/predseda-vlady-robert-fico-a-minister-vnutra-robert-kalinak-navstivili-macedonsko-%E2%80%93-grecku-hranicu

Fronc, M. (2015). *Spoločná Česko-Slovenská Digitálna parlamentná knižnica, Archív. Stenozáznam.* NRSR. https://www.nrsr.sk/dl

Galko, Ľ. (2015). *Spoločná Česko-Slovenská Digitálna parlamentná knižnica, Archív, Stenozáznam.* https://www.nrsr.sk/dl

Kačer, R. (2023). Facebook. https://www.facebook.com/rastislav.kacer

Kaliňák, R. (2016). Smer-SD Website. https://stwebsmer.strana-smer.sk

Kaník, Ľ. (2015). *Spoločná Česko-Slovenská Digitálna parlamentná knižnica, Archív, Stenozáznam.* https://www.nrsr.sk/dl

Konspiratori. https://konspiratori.sk/zoznam-stranok

Kotleba, M. (2019). *Časopis Naše Slovensko.* ĽSNS. http://www.naseslovensko.net/casopis-nase-slovensko

Kuffa, Š. (2015, June 24). *Spoločná Česko-Slovenská Digitálna parlamentná knižnica, Archív. Stenozáznam.* NRSR. https://www.nrsr.sk/dl

ĽSNS (2019). ĽSNS Website. http://www.naseslovensko.net

Mazurek, M. (2015). *Časopis Naše Slovensko.* ĽSNS. http://www.naseslovensko.net/casopis-nase-slovensko

Mazurek, M. (2023). Facebook. https://www.facebook.com/MilanMazurek. Republika

Ministry of Defence of the Slovak Republic (2021). Security Strategy of the Slovak Republic. https://www.mosr.sk/data/files/4263_210128-bezpecnos tna-strategia-sr-2021.pdf

Repulika (2023). *Program*. https://www.hnutie-republika.sk/program

Smer-SD (2022, August 25). R. Fico: slovalcu aj Duslu Šaľa by sa dalo rýchlo pomôcť zdanením bánk, R. Sulík to odmieta. *Veci verejné*. https://veci-vere jne.sk/r-fico-slovalcu-aj-duslu-sala-by-sa-dalo-rychlo-pomoct-zdanenim-bank-r-sulik-to-odmieta%EF%BF%BC/

Tlačová agentúra Slovenskej republiky (2016, February 5). Z karnevalu v Kolíne nad Rýnom hlásia sexuálne útoky a znásilnenie. *Teraz.sk*, https://www.teraz. sk/zahranicie/policia-v-koline-dostala-224-udani/180328-clanok.html

Tlačová agentúra Slovenskej republiky (2016, March 2). Toto nie je hrôza, toto je nebezpečenstvo, vyhlásil Fico po návšteve migrantov v Macedónsku. *Honline. sk*. https://hnonline.sk/slovensko/593159-toto-nie-je-hr-za-toto-je-nebezpe censtvo-vyhlasil-fico-po-navsteve-migrantov-v-macedonsku

Uhrík, M. (2023). Facebook. https://www.facebook.com/ing.milan.uhrik

Vorobelová, S. (2021, November 11). Vakcináckovia idú do finále! *Blog Hlavné správy*. https://blog.hlavnespravy.sk/28477/vakcinackovia-idu-do-finale

References

Anderson, M. (1996). *Frontiers, Territory and State Formation in the Modern World*. Cambridge: Polity Press.

Androvičová, J. (2015). Sekuritizácia migrantov na Slovensku – analýza diskurzu. *Sociológia, 47*(4), 319–339.

Androvičová, J. (2017). The migration and refugee crisis in political discourse in Slovakia: Institutionalized securitization and moral panic. *AUC Studia Territorialia, 16*(2).

Aradau, C. (2004). Security and the democratic scene: Desecuritization and emancipation. *Journal of International Relations and Development, 7*, 388–413.

Austin, J. L. (1962). *How to do things with words*. Oxford: Clarendon Press.

Baele, S. J., & Jalea, D. (2023). Twenty-five years of securitization theory: A corpus-based review. *Political Studies Review, 21*(2), 376–389.

Baele, S. J., & Thomson, C. P. (2017). An experimental agenda for securitization theory. *International Studies Review, 19*(4), 646–666.

Bain, W. (Ed.) (2006). *The Empire of Security and the Safety of the People*. New York, London: Routledge.

Bajaník, Ľ., & Frindt, M. (2022). Kríza „objektivizátorov" v televíznej žurnalistike. Spochybňovanie dôveryhodnosti respondentov v čase kríz. In A. Sámelová, M. Stanková, & J. Hacek (Eds.), *Fenomén 2022: Médiá a kríza autorít* (pp. 18–29). Bratislava: Univerzita Komenského v Bratislave.

Baldwin, D. (1997). The concept of security. *Review of International Studies, 23*(1), 5–26.

Balibar, E., & Wallerstein, I. (1992). *Rasse Klasse Nation. Ambivalente Identitäten*. Berlin: Argument Verlag.

Balzacq, T. (2005). The three faces of securitization: Political agency, audience and context. *European Journal of International Relations, 11*(2), 171–201.

Balzacq, T. (2011). A theory of securitisation: Origins, core assumptions and variants. Securitization theory. In T. Balzacq (Ed.), *Securitization Theory. How Security Problems Amerge and Dissolve* (pp. 1–30). Milton Park, Abingdon, Oxon: Routledge.

Baranov, A. (2000). Metafory v politicheskom diskurse: jazykovye markery krizisnosti politicheskoy situacii. In L. Zybatow (Ed.), *Linguistic Change in Europe: 1990-2000* (pp. 35–42). Wien: Peter Lang.

Baranov, A. (2011). *Korruptsiya: netraditsionniy vzglyad. Metaforicheskiye grani korruptsii*. Moskva: Institut Russkogo Jazyka Vinogradova.

Baranov, A. N., & Karaulov, J. N. (1994). *Slovar russkikh politicheskikh metafor.* Moskva: Pomovskii i partner.

Berger, P., & Luckmann, T. (1966). *The Social Construction of Reality: A Treatise in the Sociology of Knowledge.* Garden City, NY: Anchor Books.

Bírová, J., & Bubáková, J. (2011). Multikultúra, plurilingvizmus a preklad Charty plurilingvizmu. *XLinguae: Trimestrial European Review, 3*(4), 51–58.

Blaho, M. (2015). Manipulatívny rozmer ruského a slovenského politického diskurzu. In N. Mertová (Ed.), *Hľadanie ekvivalentností VIII* (pp. 68–73). Prešov: FF PU v Prešove.

Brezáni, J. (2023, May 23). Dvojička Smeru rastieRepublika valcuje sociálne siete, oslovuje mladých a chce vládu s Ficom a Dankom- *Postoj.* https://www. postoj.sk/130065/republika-valcuje-socialne-siete-oslovuje-mladych-a-doko nca-aj-liberalov

Burton, G., & Jirák, J. (2001). *Úvod do studia medii.* Brno: Barrister & Principal.

Busse, D., & Teubert, W. (2013). Ist Diskurs ein sprachwissenschaftliches Objekt? Zur Methodenfrage der historischen Semantik. In D. Busse, & W. Teubert (Eds.), *Linguistische Diskursnanalyse: neue Perspektiven* (pp. 13–30). Wiesbaden: Springer VS.

Buzan, B. (1991). *People, States and Fear: An Agenda for International Security Studies in the Post-Cold War Era,* 2nd edn. London: Harvester Wheatsheaf.

Buzan, B., & Hansen, L. (2009). *The Evolution of International Security Studies.* Cambridge: Cambridge University Press.

Buzan, B., & Wæver O. (2003). *Regions and Powers: The Structure of International Security.* Cambridge: Cambridge University Press.

Buzan, B., Ole Wæver, O., & De Wilde, J. (1998). *Security. A New Framework for Analysis.* Boulder, London: Lynne Rienner Publishers.

Ceyhan, A., & Tsoukala, A. (2002). The securitization of migration in western societies: Ambivalent discourses and policies. *Alternatives, 27*(1_suppl), 21–39.

Cingerová, N. (2012). Štruktúrovanie diskurzu v teórii E. Laclaua a Ch. Mouffovej a jej miesto v rámci diskurzných štúdií. *Jazyk a kultúra, 9,* 1–7.

Cingerová, N., & Dulebová, I. (2019). *Jazyk a konflikt. My a tí druhí v ruskom verejnom diskurze.* Bratislava: Univerzita Komenského v Bratislave.

Cingerová, N., Dulebová, I., & Štefančík, R. (2021). *Politická lingvistika.* Bratislava: Ekonóm.

Čermák, F. (2017). *Korpus a korpusová lingvistika.* Praha: Karolinum.

Decker, F. (2004). *Der neue Rechtspopulismus.* Opladen: Leske + Budrich.

Demirkol, A. (2023). A perspective on critical security concept and international migration Nexus through Copenhagen School: The quest for societal security. *Lectio Socialis, 7*(1), 1–10.

Denník N. (2023). *Denník N.* https://dennikn.sk /minuta/3380954

Dolník, J. (2020). Komunikačná kultúra. *Slovenská reč*, 1, 8–27.

Dugovič, T. (2023, March 3). Na Pochod za mier do Bratislavy prišli tisíce ľudí. Protestovalo sa skôr proti NATO ako proti Rusku. *Štandard.* https://standard. sk/327392/v-bratislave-sa-kona-pochod-za-mier-demonstranti-su-na-hvie zdoslavovom-namesti-prislo-niekolko-tisic-ludi-akcia-je-pokojna

Dulebová, I. (2022). Conflictogenic metaphors in R. Fico's securitisation discourse. In. R. Štefančík (Ed.), *Jazyk a politika: na pomedzí lingvistiky a politológie VII.* (pp. 76–87). Bratislava: Ekonóm.

Dulebová, I. (2021). Metaforizácia vakcinácie pri jej sekuritizácii v slovenskom politickom diskurze In R. Štefančík (Ed.), *Jazyk a politika: na pomedzí lingvistiky a politológie VI* (pp. 49–60). Bratislava: Ekonóm.

Dulebová, I., & Krajčovičová, L. (2020). Methaphorical image of Brexit in Russian media discourse (based on the methaphor of theatre). *Annales Scientia Politica, 9*(1), 18–28.

Ďurčo, P. et al. (1995). *Frazeologická terminológia.* SAV. https://www.juls.savba. sk/ediela/frazeologicka_terminologia/

Duskayeva, L. a kol. (2018). *Medialingvistika v terminach i ponatiyakh. Slovar – spravochnik.* Moskva: Flinta.

Dvorakova, K. (2016). Terminology and concepts of immigration policy in Europe and in France. *XLinguae European Scientific Language Journal, 9*(1), 2–23,

Fairclough, N. (1996). A reply to Henry Widdowson's 'Discourse analysis: A critical view'. *Language & Literature, 5*(1), 49–56.

Findra, J. (2004). *Štylistika slovenčiny.* Martin: Osveta.

Focus (2023, July 28). Volebný prieskum agentúry Focus. Sme. https://volby.sme. sk/pref/1/politicke-strany/p/focus/2023-07-28

Gajarský, L., Iermačková, O., & Spišiaková, A. (2021). Transformations of phraseological units in Russian and Slovak advertising slogans. *Filologičeskije nauki, 4*, 11–17.

Gazda, J. (2013). Jazykové prostředky řečové agrese v ruském a českém tisku. In O. Richterek, & M. Půža (Eds.), *Dialog kultur VII. Materiály z mezinárodní vědecké konference* (pp. 84–92). Hradec Králové: Gaudeamus.

Gladiš, M. (2022). Kríza autorít ako kríza komunikácie. In A. Sámelová, M. Stanková, & J. Hacek (Eds.), *Fenomén 2022: Médiá a kríza autorít* (pp. 9–18). Bratislava: Univerzita Komenského v Bratislave.

Hainsworth, P. (1992). *The Extreme Right in Europe and the USA*. New York: St Martin's Press.

Hansen, L. (2006). *Security as Practice. Discourse Analysis and the Bosnian War*. London, New York: Routledge.

Hansen, L. (2011). Theorizing the image for security studies: Visual securitization and the Muhammad Cartoon Crisis. *European Journal of International Relations, 17*(1), 51–74.

Hatoková, M. (2014). Sme pri rozhodovaní obeťami sociálnych vplyvov? In E. Ballová Mikušková, & V. Čavojová (Eds.), *Rozhodovanie v kontexte kognície, osobnosti a emócií. Súčasné trendy v rozhodovaní* (pp. 151–156). Bratislava: SAV.

Hejnal, O., & Lupták, Ľ. (2013). Využitie CAQDAS pri výskume sekuritizácie. In J. Ušiak, J. Lasicová, & D. Kollár (Eds.), *Bezpečnostné fórum 2013 – Security forum 2013* (pp. 232–239). Banská Bystrica: Fakulta politických vied a medzinárodních vzťahov Univerzita Mateja Bela v Banskej Bystrici.

Helbig, G. (1990). *Entwicklung der Sprachwissenschaft seit 1970*. Opladen: Der Westdeutsche Verlag.

Hirschová, M. (2013). *Pragmatika v češtine*. Praha: Karolinum.

Horváth, M. (2017). Uvoľnenie štýlových noriem vplyvom postmoderného diskurzu. *Slovenčinár, 4*(1), 9–15.

Hough, P. (2004). *Understanding Global Security*. New York, London: Routledge.

Hu Ch. (2023). A corpus-based study on the cognitive construction of security in discourse. *Frontiers in Psychology, 13*, 1–13.

Hutko, D. (2023, February 14). Klamstvá, strašenie aj reálne obavy. Slováci vo veľkom odopierajú vojenskú službu. *Pravda*. https://spravy.pravda.sk/dom ace/clanok/657055-vyhlasenie-o-odopreti-vykonu-mimoriadnej-sluzby-pod alo-vyse-40-tisic-obcanov

Huysmans, J. (2000). Contested community: Migration and the question of the political in the EU. In M. Kelstrup, & M. C. Williams (Eds.), *International Relations Theory and the Politics of European Integration. Power, Security and Community* (pp. 149–170). London, New York: Routledge.

Chudinov, A. (2001). *Rossiya v metaforicheskom zerkale: Kognitivnoye issledovaniye politicheskoy metafori*. Yekaterinburg: Ural State Pedagogical University.

Chudinov, A. P. (2013). *Ocherki po sovremennoy politicheskoy metaforologii*. Yekaterinburg: Ural State Pedagogical University.

International Organization for Migration, Slovakia (2022, December 31). *Migrácia na Slovensku*. https://www.iom.sk/sk/migracia/migracia-na-sloven sku.html

Islamonline.sk (2020, January 20). Zverejnili údaje zo sčítania obyvateľov. K islamu sa prihlásilo 3862 moslimov. *Islamonline.sk*. https://www.islamonline. sk/2022/01/zverejnili-udaje-zo-scitania-obyvatelov-k-islamu-sa-prihlasilo-3862-moslimov

Jasinská, L. (2019). *Hovorové lexémy v publicistických textoch*. Košice: UPJŠv Košiciach.

Karyotis, G. (2007). European migration policy in the aftermath of September 2001. The security – migration nexus. *Innovation, 20*(1): 1–17.

Kirchhoff, S. (2010). *Krieg mit Methaphern. Mediendiskurse über 9/11 und den „War onTerror"*. Bielefeld: transcript Verlag.

Korotych, V. (2016). Zoomorphic metaphor as a mean of creation of an image of the Enemy in the Ukrainian Press of 1941–1945. *Studia-linguistica*, 9.

Krupa, V. (1990). *Metafora na rozhraní vedeckých disciplín*. Bratislava: Tatran.

Kyseľ, T. (2023, Febraury 13). Padol rekord: viac ako 40-tisíc mužov odmietlo bojovať za Slovensko. *Aktuality.sk*. https://www.aktuality.sk/clanok/dXLDt83/padol-rekord-viac-ako-40-tisic-muzov-odmietlo-bojovat-za-slovensko-nad-vini-aj-fica-s-blahom

Laclau, E., & Mouffe, C. (1985). *Hegemony and Socialist Strategy*. London: Verso.

Lazaridis, G., & Tsagkroni, V. (2015). Securitisation of migration and far right populist othering in Scandinavian countries. In G. Lazaridis, & K. Wadia (Eds.), *The Securitisation of Migration in the EU Debates Since 9/11*(pp. 207–236). London: Palgrave Macmillan.

Leech, G. N. (2000). Grammar of spoken English. New outcomes of corpus-oriented research. *Language Learning, 50*(4), 675–724.

Letavajová, S. (2018). *Zmiešané manželstvá (manželstvá s cudzincami ako sociokultúrny fenomén)*. Nitra: UKF v Nitre.

Letavajová, S., Chlebcová Hečková A., Krno S., & Bošelová M. (2020). Novodobé migrácie vo verejnej, mediálnej a politickej diskusii. Nitra. Filozofická fakulta Univerzita Konštantína Filozofa v Nitre.

Liďák, J. (2014). International migration, Europe and migration from Africa. *Asian and African Studies, 23*(2), 226–254.

Martinovský, P. (2016). *Environmentální bezpečnost v České republice*. Brno: Masarykova univerzita

McDonald, M. (2008). Securitization and the construction of security. *European Journal of International Relations, 14*(4), 563–587.

Mesežnikov G., & Bartoš J. (2021). *Kto hrá ruskú ruletu na Slovensku*. Bratislava: Inštitút pre verejné otázky.

MIPEX (2020). *Slovakia*. MIPEX. https://www.mipex.eu/slovakia

Molnárová, E. (2013). *Spoločensko-politická lexika z kontrastívneho aspektu.* Banská Bystrica: Belianum, FHV UMB.

Molnárová, E., & Lauková, J. (2018). *Jazykový obraz migrácie v nemeckom masmediálnom diskurze.* Banská Bystrica: Belianum.

Morozov, V. (2009). *Rossia i drugie: identichnost i granicy politicheskogo soobshchestva.* Moskva: NLO.

Murphy, L. M., & Koskela, A. (2010). *Key Terms in Semantics.* London, New York: Continuum International Publishing Group.

Nowak, A., Szamrej, J., & Latané, B. (1990). From private attitude to public opinion: A dynamic theory of social impact. *Psychological Review, 97*(3), 362–376.

Pörksen, B. (2000). *Die Konstruktion von Feindbildern. Zum Sprachgebrauch vonneonazistischen Medien.* Wiesbaden: Westdeutscher Verlag.

Riaposova A. (2002). *Metaforicheskiye modeli s agressivnym pragmaticheskim potentsialom.*

Rozhlas a televízia Slovenska (2022, March 23). *Ruská sociálna sieť Telegram je útočiskom pre slovenské dezinformačné weby.* RTVS. https://spravy.rtvs.sk/2022/03/ruska-socialna-siet-telegram-je-utociskom-pre-slovenske-dezinformacne-weby/

Sakalauskaite, A. (2010). *Zoometaphors in English, German, and Lithuanian: A Corpus Study.* Berkeley: University of California, Berkeley.

Sámelová, A. (2020). Online komunity ako producenti mediálnych obsahov. In A. Sámelová, M. Stanková, & J. Hacek, J. (Eds.), *Fenomén 2020: komunita v mediálnom priestore* (pp. 18–26). Bratislava: Univerzita Komenského v Bratislave.

Sámelová, A. (2022). Fenomén 2022: Médiá a kríza autorít. In A. Sámelová, M. Stanková, & J. Hacek (Eds.), *Fenomén 2022: Médiá a kríza autorít* (pp. 6–8). Bratislava: Univerzita Komenského v Bratislave.

Shapiro, M. J. (1989). Textualizing global politics. In J. Der Derian, & J. M. Shapiro (Eds.), *International/Intertextual Relations: Postmodern Readings of World Politics* (pp. 11–23). New York: Lexington Books.

Schneier, B. (2008). The psychology of security. In S. Vaudenay (Ed.), *AFRICACRYPT 2008, LNCS 5023* (pp. 50–79). Heidelberg: Springer-Verlag.

Skačan, J. (2017). Critical analysis of media discourse: Islam, Jihad and Islamophobia. *Philosophica Critica, 3*(2), 15–33.

Sklyarevskaya, G. N. (1993). *Metaphor in the System of Language.* Sankt Peterburg: Nauka.

Sommer R., & Sommer B. (2011). Zoomorphy: Animal metaphors for human personality. *Antropozoos, 24*(3), 237–248.

Spišiaková, M., & Mocková, N. (2022). Colours in politics in Spanish speaking countries. *Folia Linguistica et Litteraria: Časopis za nauku o jeziku i književnosti*, 39, 273–294.

Spitzmüller, J., & Warnke, I. H. (2011). *Diskurslinguistik. Eine Einführung in Theorien und Methoden der transtextuellen Sprachanalyse.* Berlin, Boston: Walter de Gruyter.

Stritzel, H. (2007). Towards a theory of securitization: Copenhagen and beyond. *European Journal of International Relations*, 13(3), 357–383.

Stritzel, H. (2014). *Security in Translation Securitization Theory and the Localization of Threat.* Basingstoke: Palgrave Macmillan.

Struhárik, F. (2023, July 4). Fico vyhráva na Facebooku, Smeru sa darí aj na TikToku. Instagram je úplne iný svet. *Denník N.* https://dennikn.sk/3456131/fico-vyhrava-na-facebooku-smeru-sa-dari-aj-na-tiktoku-instagram-je-uplne-iny-svet

Štatistické sčítanie obyvateľov, domov a bytov (2021). Náboženské vyznanie. https://www.scitanie.sk/k-rimskokatolickemu-vyznaniu-sa-prihlasilo-56-obyvatelov

Šnídl, V. (2017). *Pravda a lož na Facebooku.* Bratislava: N Press s.r.o.

Štefančík, R. (2020). Metafora vojny v jazyku politiky. *Lingua et Vita*, 17, 59–69.

Štefančík, R. (2022). *Radikálny populizmus v ére pandémie COVID-19 a vojny na Ukrajine.* Bratislava: Ekonóm.

Štefančík, R., & Dulebová, I. (2017). *Jazyk a politika. Jazyk politiky v konfliktnej štruktúre spoločnosti.* Bratislava: Ekonóm.

Štefančík, R., & Dulebová, I. (2017). Securitization theory of the Copenhagen school from the perspective of discourse analysis and political linguistics. *XLinguae Journal*, 10(2), 51–62.

Štefančík, R., Némethová, I., & Seresová, T. (2021). Securitisation of migration in the language of Slovak far-right populism. *Migration Letters*, 18(6), 731–744.

Šušol et al. (2012). *Informačná politika.* 2. vydanie. Bratislava: STIMUL.

Takács, D. (2021, November 8). Slovenské dezinformačné weby ako piliere proruských naratívov na Slovensku. Infosecurity.sk. https://infosecurity.sk/dezinfo/slovenske-dezinformacne-weby-ako-piliere-proruskych-narativov-na-slovensku/

Taylor, Ch. (2021). Metaphors of migration over time. *Discourse & Society*, 32(4), 463–481.

Thompson, S. (1996). Politics without metaphors is like a fish without water. In J. S. Mio, & A. N. Katz (Eds), *Metaphor: Implications and Applications* (pp. 185–201). Mahwah, NJ: Lawrence Erlbaum Associates.

Tlačová agentúra Slovenskej republiky, TASR (2023, July 28). Prieskum: Matovičova koalícia by do parlamentu neprešla, SNS aj SaS tesne áno. *Sme.* https://domov. sme.sk/c/23199219/prieskum-politickych-stran-jul-focus-2023.html

Tóth, G. (2023, Febuary 19). Smer vie, ako na to! Fico suverénne ovládol sociálne siete, Matovičovi ostanú len oči pre plač. *Plus 1 Deň.* https://www1.pluska. sk/spravy/z-domova/smer-vie-ako-to-fico-suverenne-ovladol-socialne-siete-matovicovi-ostanu-len-oci-pre-plac

Troszyński, M., & El-Ghamari, M. (2022). A great divide: Polish media discourse on migration, 2015–2018. *Humanities and Social Sciences Communications, 9,* 1–12.

Ullman, R. (1983). Redefining security. *International Security, 8*(1), 129–153.

Ušiak, J., & Nečas, P. (2011). Societálny a politický sektor v kontexte bezpečnosti štátu. *Politické vedy, 14*(1), 30–49.

Vershinina, T. (2002). *Zoomorfnaya, fitomorfnaya i antropomorfnaya metafora v sovremennom politicheskom diskurse.*

Višňovský, J., & Prašovská, P. (2022) Pandémia falošných správ v čase pandémie covidu-19 alebo ktorým falošným správam a hoaxom veríme. In A. Sámelová, M. Stanková, & J. Hacek (Eds.), *ENOMÉN 2022: Médiá a kríza autorít* (pp. 93–107). Bratislava: Univerzita Komenského v Bratislave.

Voroshilova M. & Pashkova, A. D. (2016). *Kreolizirovannaya metafora kak orudiye diskreditatsii.* Politicheskaya lingvistika, 2016, No. 6, 91–95.

Wæver, O. (2000). The EU as a security actor: Reflections from a pessimistic constructivist on post-sovereign security orders. In M. Kelstrup, & M. Williams (Eds), *International Relations Theory and the Politics of European Integration: Power, Security, and Community* (pp. 250–294). London: Routledge.

Wæver, O. (2007). Securitization and desecuritization. In B. Buzan, & L. Hansen (Eds.), *International Security* (pp. 66–98). Vol. 3. Widening Security. Los Angeles et al.: SAGE.

Zahorák A. (2022). *Precedentné fenomény ako nástroj v interpretácii prekladového umeleckého textu.* Nitra: Univerzita Konštantína Filozofa v Nitre.

Zajonc, R. B. (1980). Feeling and thinking: Preferences need no inferences. *American Psychologist, 35,* 151–175.

Zimenová, Z. (2019, January 10). O bordeli, dievčatách a posteliach alebo keď hrubosť formuje realitu. *Blog Sme.* https://dennikn.sk/blog/1345949/o-bord eli-dievcatach-a-posteliach-alebo-ked-hrubost-formuje-realitu

Zouhar, M. (2022). *Argument: nástroj myslenia a presviedčania.* Bratislava: VEDA SAV.

Studies in Linguistics, Anglophone Literatures and Cultures

Edited by Robert Kiełtyka and Agnieszka Uberman